THE UNCERTAIN SOUND

*If the trumpet give forth an uncertain sound
who will prepare himself for battle?*
                                    1 Cor 14:8

The Uncertain Sound

BY JOHN H. McGOEY, S.F.M.

THE BRUCE PUBLISHING COMPANY/MILWAUKEE

Foreword

THIS book will be only one of many published in the aftermath of Vatican II, manifesting the eagerness of the clergy to involve itself in the business of the Church. Some of the things said may sound harsh; others, perhaps, unreasonable; certainly, some of the opinions expressed may be wrong. However, nothing is said mischievously, maliciously, thoughtlessly, or without respect for the Church I believe to be God's, or without solicitude for those I believe to be the people of God.

The pressure to produce this book came from secular priests, pastors, grateful to God and the Church for being such. They have no desire to heap abuse upon the Church, or upon those, however frail, who are charged with the grave responsibility of guiding its destiny. However, they believe that Christ's obvious and frequent disappointment in His apostles was not expressed so clearly in the Gospels by accident, nor was the inspired revelation of their weakness inadvertent or imprudent, let alone uncharitable. They believe the humanity of the Church to be at once its strength and its weakness, insuring its very human administrators against personal inflation, and making their dependence on God an obvious necessity.

It seems to them that those responsible for the direction of the Church should be the first to see and admit their failings. It seems that those who publicly profess their love of God should indeed be lovers of the truth, more generous than others in their efforts to accomplish the human perfection of the Church. Nor does it seem without significance that the outstanding harshness of Christ in the Gospels, and perhaps His only harshness, is against hypocrisy, the willful blindness of those claiming leadership in the name of God. Hypocrisy is man's use of the things of God for his own glory. It is too frequently the specialty of churchmen.

The priests anxious for this book met to explore its possibility. Despite knowing that no book receives unanimous approval, and that the capacity of writers is limited by their intelligence, experience, and many other imponderables, they want the book produced because:

They believe there is a need for such a book now.

They believe that in the surprising call for a council by Pope John XXIII the Holy Spirit was at work and that a new and glorious hope of progress was being held out.

They believe that although their opinions have not been earnestly sought, they, as pastors, have opinions which can come from neither the bishops nor the laity.

They believe that, in the innumerable discussions in countless rectories by interested priests, there are good things said and heard to which neither the bishops nor the laity are party.

They believe that, since the sole purpose of the Church is to lead men to God, their work as pastors is of the essence. And so the changes they think should take place in the Church to accomplish this purpose make up much of the material of this book.

After some discussion it was decided that the book would be the work of one man, fed by the thoughts and recommendations of the others. I was asked to be that man, and I take full responsibility for what is said, as I must do. However, the others support me as fully as, in all honesty, they can, and accept their share of the responsibility.

I do not insist that I am right, nor that there is any final or complete answer in what I say. I claim only that I am as right as I know how to be, and that I have not deliberately exaggerated nor been hypercritical.

To make sure that the opinions expressed are not mine alone, a questionnaire was set up and given a wide geographical distribution. I wanted the opinions of others to guide my thinking, or at least prevent my being ridiculous. The material of the questionnaire makes up an appendix to the book. It should be interesting enough even to those for whom statistics mean as little as perhaps they should. There is no pretense that the answers to the questionnaire have not influenced me to an appreciable degree. But that is not altogether bad.

And so the book is presented for what it is worth, and I accept gladly any criticism which may ensue.

Contents

Foreword   v

1   What History Could Teach Us   1

2   Priests and the Priesthood   23

3   Vocations and the Seminaries   64

4   Communications   89

5   Reorganization of the Administration   107

6   Priests and Parish Work   118

7   Canon Law   140

8   The Liturgy   153

9   Catholic Education   166

10   The Church and Money   181

11   The Foreign Missions   194

12   Freedom of Conscience   202

13   The Diaspora   207

Conclusion   209

The Questionnaire   215

THE UNCERTAIN SOUND

Chapter 1

What History Could Teach Us

IF CHURCH history is a record of the love of God for men and the protection Christ promised His apostles as they in anguish watched His final parting from them, it is also the unenviable record of the failures of Christians, who without Him could do nothing and many times have done much worse than nothing. Certainly there is little evidence in history to show that men have learned much from the past. George Wilhelm Hegel put it very well when he said, "What experience and history teach is this: that people and governments have never learned anything from history, or acted on principles deduced from it." Put another way, it can be said, "He who does not read history destines history to repeat itself." With Vatican II now closed and the world looking forward to the changes which could follow it, there must be found some reason to hope that man's penchant for repeating his mistakes will diminish. It must not be concluded that he simply cannot learn from his mistakes. It would be a supertragedy to have to do so in the case of the administration of the Church, which is, like it nor not, the moral force in the world. Surely when

1

each of man's mechanical inventions is constantly improved or replaced by a more efficient invention, there must be some hope that man himself from generation to generation can do a little better than his predecessors.

Without the least pretense of scholarship, one could present many historic events of the last thousand years in the hope of avoiding similar mistakes with equally unfortunate consequences. For the events used to illustrate this point there will be little detail and no footnotes, no bibliography. One can read about these events in any of the available and reliable versions of the historic record. Truly, too much of recorded history has been the work of partisan writers or the paid diarists of interested parties to the various disputes, contentions, and schisms. Still, today we are the beneficiaries of the studious labors of historians trying for as objective a version as possible of the conflicts of men. Study or even cursory reading of these cannot but contribute toward harmonious living among men of various races, nations, and religions.

Scholarly men today, in a way unknown before, are genuinely seeking truth, honestly contending with their acknowledged human bias. In the respect of these scholars for the truth, tools are being found for the reconciliation so desperately needed by a world which cannot much longer afford the luxury of serious animosities. The present challenges to the continued existence of men on earth plainly demand a unity of purpose and endeavor. No realist can excuse himself from the effort toward human solidarity. Man can only hope that the pursuit of the truth in history will produce the understanding and the empathy required for all men to work for peace — not toward a peace which will merely leave him more time to indulge his appetites for pleasure and enjoyment, but the peace which will provide the time and inspiration to build a world in which the good things of this earth are shared more equitably by all. It is so obvious that senseless divisive factors in society threaten to make a living hell out of a world which is filled with riches and beauty enough for heaven.

Few knowledgeable people deny that the great religious schisms of the last thousand years of Christianity would have been quite unnecessary, had the personalities involved taken the time and had the coolness to sit down and discuss their differences with intelligence and goodwill. There were wrongs on all sides which dispassionate and good men could have seen and would willingly have righted. They did not do so through their own perversity as well as through the fault of poor communications, reports of things which never happened and quotations of statements never uttered. Yet today, so many of the ingredients required for schisms and for wars are simply nonexistent. It is a tribute to man's inherent desire for peace that two such powerful and potentially destructive antagonists as the United States and Russia can consent to a "hot-line" always open to any message which could keep impetuosity or misunderstanding from leading to the holocaust of modern war. It is a disappointing but happy fact that this "hot-line" preceded the "cool-line" now opening between men of religion, men of peace, followers of the One who came to bring peace to the world, but who have so often settled their differences with the sword in the very name of the God of love.

Regardless of how religious men may be, they always remain human. They have to deal daily with their human weaknesses and particularly with the selfishness which makes any man want to have things his own way. However, there is more evidence than ever before that no one can do as he wishes just because he wishes. The man who will learn from history can plainly see the line he ought to take if historic disaster is not to be his continual companion.

Consider first the great schism which took place in the Church between East and West at the end of the first Christian millenium. Volumes have been written without obscuring, beyond redemption, certain basic facts. There is simply no weighty evidence that Photius, who through generations of history was by western minds made the archvillain in the case, was ever hostile to the Holy See. In fact it can be authoritatively stated that Photius, at the time of his death, was in communion with Rome. And it is more and more evident that this rift between the East and the West was originally opened by one of the two factions warring within the Byzantine Church itself. This faction for its own ends won the favor of Pope Nicholas by falsely denouncing Photius. When the final rift was made inevitable by the papal bull excommunicating Patriarch Michael Caerularius in 1054 (which was lifted only in 1965), the bull was placed upon the altar of Sancta Sophia only after Leo IX, who issued it, had been dead since the previous July 16, rendering the bull invalid. Today, communications being what they are, the parties to such a difference would likely be discussing the matter face to face in a common meeting place. Perhaps communications and the jet age had more to do with the embrace of Paul VI and Athenagoras in Jerusalem than did any difference between these two men and their antecedents, Nicholas and Photius.

So eager are men in our day for arbitration rather than for war that they will compel it. Examples of this are the carefully guarded peace in Cyprus, the UN supervision in the Congo or along the Israeli-Jordan border. While it cannot be denied that Jordan and Syria remain quite hostile to the newly established Israel, it can be denied that their hostility is uncontrollable. It is too evident that the self-interest of the greater powers is making peace not only possible but mandatory. Had such conditions prevailed in times past, the pilgrims' passports to the holy places would have been authorized, not by the blood of the crusaders' swords, but rather, if not by one man's respect for the religious sentiment of another, at least by mutual dependence on the tourist trade. Not that the elements for war are lacking in the world today; it is simply harder for the elements of peace to be eliminated by any one man's impetuous distemper.

The second consideration is of Martin Luther and the reformers. Considering this event, one can again see how much the times in which the trouble took place contributed to four hundred years and more of estrangement between groups of people equally insistent on their love for the same God. History has made clear to its dispassionate readers that there were momentous wrongs, misconceptions, ignorance, and bad will on both sides of the Reformation action. There was not then sufficient time lapse between mind, emotion, and muscle to make thoughtful consideration of the issues a factor in the conflict. Nor was there, for all concerned, easy access to a place of parley, had they been so disposed. Neither could Catholic authority conceive the possibility of righteous grievance nor the Protestant side the possibility of reasonable appeal.

Although it has taken four hundred years of mellowing and some regret to do it, a strange thing has happened. Vatican II has made conservative Catholics fearful that the protestantizing of the Church has begun, and conservative Protestants afraid that catholicization of Protestantism has begun. Most Catholics have learned that Luther's story is more than that of an apostate monk running off with a nun. Protestants have learned that, had today's spirit of reform swept the Church in Luther's time, his personal problems would have been his only ones. Now many great and good things Luther fought and suffered for are part of Catholic life, and many accretions he fought against have been abandoned. Both sides are now closer to agreeing that the only acceptable answer to any problem is the truth.

It is an unfortunately late luxury, but a real luxury nevertheless, to consider what might have been, had the words of Adrian VI to the Imperial Diet assembled at Nuremberg in 1552 been given the prominence before the world that the words of reconciliation of Paul VI in 1964 and 1965 were given by radio, television, and the Telstar satellite. For Adrian's words surely showed a goodness and an openness of mind and heart not excelled by Paul VI, although the means of transmitting them were such that even now, some four hundred years later, too few have gotten his message. So clear and pointed were his words that, in relation to a situation vastly different and incredibly less explosive, they could be misconstrued as controversial and discriminatory, perhaps too dangerous and too true to be risked in the drama of reconciliation. Adrian's document said in part: "We freely confess that God permits this persecution of His Church because of the sins of men, particularly those of priests and prelates. . . . All these evils have perhaps originated with the Roman Curia."

While partisan historians, as wrong objectively as they were subjectively self-righteous, have left a legacy of understandable but unfortunate distortions, it is quite possible that such an event as the Reformation might well be avoided today. Many thoughtful scholars, with no claims to infallibility, but with large claims to credibility, have said it could be so. Regardless of cultural and scientific developments and the progress of grace in the souls of men, man remains free to throw a wrench into the best plans of his fellows. However, doing so will seem progressively less sensible as the consequences of such an act become more evident. More effective application of Christian revelation to men's lives, and the greater practice of virtue by those of position in the Church, will make those consequences more evident and the alternatives even more desirable.

The sagas of the foreign mission expeditions to Asia of three hundred years ago provide the next two episodes showing the power of human weakness to obliterate human heroism. The smallness of men of pride in right, rather than the greatness of men of humility and love, colored the following two centuries of Christian frustration and irreparable loss to the Church. One of the staggering facts of history is the penchant of "good" men professing to love and serve the longsuffering Christ, and pledged to a life of virtue by the public profession of religious vows, to fight each other for the privilege of carrying the "good news" of Christ to pagan nations. The strange doctrine of esprit de corps loyalty to men, rather than to Christ, too thinly coated their personal pride. This veneer made it quite easy for them to insist that loyalty to their holy founders and their respective congregations made holy what amounted to a crusade against one another. Yet each religious order was ostensibly engaged in the same work to the same end, which unity in charity could have achieved. Surely modern men of a small degree of common sense and a little virtue must see how ridiculous such a posture was even in the eyes of pagans. To carry on such a vendetta in the name of Christ would be blasphemous were it not so patently ridiculous.

The historic days of the foreign missions to the heathen (as he was condescendingly called, though many pagans were better people than their would-be deliverers from darkness and depravity) are replete with legends of praise for the Church. But the Church would certainly have made more progress had the praise been more often earned or deserved. In the real history of this legendary heroism, hardly equalled in the annals of mankind, there was ample evidence of living which was truly Christian and which could solve the problems of disharmony and confusion racking the Church today, if it were lived again and let prevail instead of being crushed.

In the great work in India of Roberto de Nobili, one of the early Italian Jesuits (largely overlooked because those times were historically Portuguese), there is an epic of devotion to Jesus Christ. Yet this young man's work was halted and almost obliterated in the name of Jesus Christ. By invoking obedience to cover their envy, superiors unequal to his dedication, lacking his clarity of vision and his understanding of

the Indian culture, rejoiced in bringing to an end the apostolic
work of a giant. Self-righteously they deprived the pagan of
the chance to assay the truth for himself, which he was
capable of doing by the fact that he too was destined by
creation to be a child of God. The foreign mission work in
every nation is marked by a superiority complex in the missionary, a thinly veiled and deeply resented contempt for the
"natives" — and this mostly because of their lack of material
power, luxury, technology, and wealth. It is all too human,
though not very Christian, to be contemptuous of those who
do not share one's own advantages. But when the representatives of the Church bless the humanity of doing so and make
nationalism a virtue, giving to nations a messianic mission, the
honest pagan reasonably loses sight of the Christianity and
sees imperialism. The history of the missions has been a
record of good, well-meaning men confusing patriotism with
Christianity, national supremacy with the blessing of almighty
God, and power with a wisdom given an aura of heaven,
however earthly it may have been.

Had the ways and works of Roberto de Nobili been studied
and imitated, had his success not created such envy in the
hearts of those coveting his success, there would be a flourish-
ing and influential Christian Church in India today — one
not won by muscle and the sword but by the efficacious power
of goodness and the truth.

This man, like so many others before him, was condemned
by authority so sure that it was operating in the name and
place of God that it was blind to its dreadful representation
of God. He won the respect of the Indian people and was
given the title of "guru," teacher, but he could not please the
superiors who had given him the task he did so well. Anxious
to have his way, De Nobili's provincial saw no wrong in re-
wording the superior general's obedience to De Nobili to
suit his own commands. Thus Roberto was forbidden to bap-
tize a single convert for a two-year period, during which he

was left to languish under the shadow of disobedience. Surely superiors really convinced that they stand in the place of God should sometimes be caught trembling, but never haughty or impervious to the truth. Nor should any human instrument in his conviction of the divinity of God lose sight of his own humanity, or be forgetful of how easily this can happen to those wearing the mantle of authority. This has been a great difficulty in the Church. Despite the fact that only one man has been declared infallible, and that in a very restricted sense under conditions seldom present and for declarations relatively few, the aura of infallibility seems deceptively close to those who participate in any small degree in that one man's administration. Nor can collegiality, so unfortunately left undeclared in Vatican I by force of circumstances but declared in Vatican II, bring personal infallibility to any bishop or superior.

The story of the magnificent Mateo Ricci is equally impressive. This apostle left an indelible mark in the history of the missions. He had such an understanding of and insight into a way of life so foreign to his own that his work stands almost alone in its profundity. His genius, zeal, and achievements opened China to him and thus to Christ as never before. Yet they were unremarkable and unacceptable to lesser religious as equally blind to his greatness as to their own limitations. Had Ricci's marvelous accomplishments been admitted as quickly by the Church as they were by the Chinese pagan scholars impressed by his ascetic scholarship, there might not have been a Communist regime in China today. Nor do those who were privileged to work in that large and populous kingdom in later years question for a moment that, had Mateo Ricci had his way, the contribution of China to Christianity would have been of inestimable value. Although fortunately there are extant sufficiently adequate records of what took place to warrant his complete vindication, it took other men three hundred years to tell the world that he was right and they were wrong. When those responsible for the suppression of this man's work are claimants to the custodianship of truth and responsibility for bringing the good tidings to the world, the implications are as obvious as the history is unfortunate.

Certainly there is little to be gained by the continuous castigation of those whose fault it was that such a thing took place. But the cause for rejoicing, that we at last know the truth, should not obscure a firm purpose of amendment. The truth ought always to inspire in us a willingness to doubt our omniscience and to give the ideas of other dissenters the hearing they warrant.

One could go on indefinitely dredging up incidents of human weakness which make history an embarrassment to those unduly proud of the management of Christ's Church. However, only two more are selected, virtually from our own times. And it should be noted here that history can have as convenient a memory as the recorder of it, and time can make a gross injustice appear as an honest mistake when historians will have it so. It is this inconsistency which allows those who stoned the prophets to claim credit for their sanctity because the persecutions made them saints. Building monuments to the prophets is a very worthy undertaking, but it does not change the fact that the same builders' hands put an end to the haunting message God sent the prophets to give. The real atonement for the injustice wrought upon so many of the saints by those to whom they were sent lies in the efficacious purpose of not forcing history to repeat itself.

The story of Isaac Hecker, or "Yankee Paul" as he is called by one of his biographers, is filled with the kind of incident referred to by Christ when He told His apostles that those who persecuted them and put them to death would think they were rendering a service to God. Hecker was an intellectual American convert of the early nineteenth century who ultimately founded the Paulist Fathers. He was the victim of that nationalism so common in history which made pride of nation second only to personal pride in impeding Christian living. When he considered himself called to the priesthood he joined the Redemptorist Fathers. They were primarily German, as were so many other immigrants to America of that time. It was no surprise that Hecker himself was accused of nationalism when, in an English-speaking country, with an English-speaking apostolate before him, he requested that English be the language spoken in the houses. He was self-righteously condemned for making such a request and told in no uncertain terms that German would continue to be the language of the religious houses of the order in America. It seems impossible that it would not have dawned on these would-be good men that their insistence on German might be equally nationalistic.

Thus it did not seem incongruous to the superior when he was leaving America for the general chapter of the order in Rome that he should appoint as acting superior a man who was manifestly insane, but German. So aware was the provincial of this fact that he gave a letter to another member of the order instructing him to take charge in the event the interim-superior went mad. This man was also German. Within a few days of the provincial's departure for the Eternal City, the acting superior did go mad. This all happened without the provincial's sense of failure in the training of the young American religious who were, despite all evidence to the contrary, considered incapable of taking charge as adequately as a madman. How reasonable the astonishment at the failure of such good men to be objective in their dealings with their subjects, or to treat them with charity. Thoughtful inquirers must be puzzled as to why such godly men can consider themselves the instruments of God in inflicting these humiliations on their subjects, calculated to inculcate humility. The obvious contradiction of such an action to the teachings of Christ was clearly not obvious to them. Nor did it dawn on them that they were making the end justify the means. No man really has a right before God to inflict humiliation on his fellowman and call it charity. Yet this has been a practice in much of the formation of religious.

Hecker's convictions ultimately led him before the San-hedrin of authority. He found himself in Rome earnestly de-fending those convictions, still convinced that he wished to be no more than a good Redemptorist. How often an aura of benevolence has been given by historians to those requiring the all but endless and unendurable sojourns in Rome of good men trying to clear themselves of blame they did not deserve, for things they did not do. In the twisted effort to "uphold authority," how many unworthy steps were taken in the name of God? Certainly the unremitting effort to impress subjects with their power of authority was not much akin to the forbearance of Jesus Christ when He was challenged.

Isaac Hecker was a good man, quite content with the religious order of his choice. Undoubtedly he would have been another ornament in its record. However, he was dis-missed from the order because he would not see where he was wrong when he was really right. How often superiors are tolerant of the man who could not care less for their authority, and punish the one who respects them but finds himself in honest disagreement with them. The only expla-nation must be that those who care little for authority con-demn themselves by their actions, whereas those who respect authority but disagree with its decisions heap contumely on superiors by their upright lives. So often the priest who is a libertine, an alcoholic, or coldly indifferent to his obliga-tions will be tolerated much more than the priest who questions the wisdom of a decision of authority. The dis-missal of Isaac Hecker from the Redemptorist Order, despite his earnest wishes to the contrary, forced him to found a new order of secular priests which, despite minor variations, does virtually the same work as the Redemptorists.

The proliferation of religious orders doing each other's work has generally been precipitated by disagreement among good men. The cases of this are too numerous to specify. In the work of establishment and progress the new orders are forced to repeat almost all the mistakes of the parent order, and then still retain in themselves the same human weaknesses and deficiencies. And by some spiritual or intellectual magic this is made to look like the will of God, through whose providence these things are supposed to redound to His honor and glory, the growth and development of the Church. Strange that so many in authority have called for the reunion of the Protestants and other heretics with the parent church and yet seldom have called the offshoot religious orders to rejoin their parent orders and try once more to work together for the honor and glory of God. One seems as logical as the other, and yet the former is so much easier to accept and understand. Popular theology would make it appear that efficiency and work well done just cannot show forth the greatness of God as can division, strife, and almost every form of human folly. To see these things as inevitable is one thing; to bless them in the name of God is another. Yet it has been widely done.

The principle "charity over all" has been stressed from time immemorial. Christ himself could not have been clearer when asked about the great commandment of the law. It was, He said, that a man should love God with his whole heart and mind, and then he should love his neighbor as himself. In this consisted, according to Christ, "the whole law and the prophets." Yet it remains a fact that in many if not most ecclesiastical courts the least stipulation of the law carries more weight than does charity. Well might the world shake its head at such a patent contradiction between teaching and practice.

Nowhere is the legal aspect of the Church more in evidence than when a religious society goes into a mission territory to work. The society must sign a legal contract with the bishop governing the work. If charity does not bind a bishop to a religious society and its men and work, will a paper document do so? If charity does not inspire the men entering a mission territory to do their best work for God and souls, will a legal document do so? Yet these instruments of the courts are taken seriously in the Church. This rigid inflexibility governing the Church from the legal point of view has had, as mentioned above, the remarkable effect of making life in religion more tolerable for the public sinner and even the renegade than it has for the zealous apostolic man. Why should not a priest intent on good work, who knows what he wants to do, and has shown prudent judgment and true zeal, be allowed to give himself fully to such work? Why should it be necessary that he waste years of his life, ergs of his energy, and the bulk of his talents in the processes of vindication, or the establishment of an administration duplicating wasteful extravagances of already existing facilities? Much of the world laughed at the Communists in China for the incredibly stupid adventure in homesite blast furnaces for the production of steel by the peasantry, but the same thing has often been done in the Church through the useless proliferation of religious orders, primarily because there is so little outlet for the zeal of good men and women under the existing restrictions. They must go through complicated formalities and await ruefully granted dispensations rather than receive a simple blessing. A hundred years after the death of "Yankee Paul" it may well be asked if there was really any point in forcing him to establish the Paulists, or what kind of minds forced him to such extremes to prove the justice of his cause.

The final example of unnecessary historic tragedy is Father Vincent Lebbe. He was the man who did so much to bring the Church in China back into repute following the Boxer

Rebellion. Under God he was more responsible for the establishment of the Chinese hierarchy than any other man save the pope who approved it. That the Chinese hierarchy was established one hundred years later than it should have been, just in time for the Communist take-over and the expulsion of the Church from that unhappy land, may well be used by some historians, if they continue in their tragic pattern, to explain the failure of the Chinese hierarchy. Yet had Mateo Ricci been listened to, and not been the victim of his detractors within the Church itself, the situation might never have developed. And even after this unfortunate occurrence, had Vincent Lebbe been heard with the respect he so surely deserved, rather than punished for his success in spreading Christianity which made those responsible for the apostolate appear inadequate and bumbling, the situation might still have been salvaged.

After bringing more than ten thousand people into the Church in Tientsin alone, he was banished from the countryside he knew so well and where he had worked so efficiently to the city of Hangchow, where he was a stranger and an outcast. The authorities of the Church in China had little good to say for this man, but at his death in 1939 the Chinese government flew all the flags in the country at halfmast. Considering the innate antiforeignism of a country which had much reason to be antiforeign, this was a fantastic tribute to a foreigner. Again, the honest pagan could see the good which escaped the willfully blinded Christian.

Surprisingly, the bishops opposing the things that Father Lebbe stood for insisted that the Chinese clergy, after decades under their tutelage, was incapable of assuming even such modest responsibility as pastorates, without seeing that they were candidly admitting their own failure as administrators. It is the failures who can least afford to admit the success of others, for they are never disposed to the contrasts which focus attention on their own mistakes. The inability of people generally to admit their mistakes is an accepted human failing. However, the tragic inability of Christian leaders to see, let alone admit, their mistakes has led, not so much to recognition of their humanity, as to the conviction by the world that Christianity itself has been a failure. It has not been able to profoundly influence its own leadership.

When those whose profession is the truth can be so easily blinded by egoism, vanity, and inflation, the truth is indeed elusive. Christ's teaching was not intended to change the nature of a man, but it certainly was intended to enable him to change his ways. But when good men manage to change perhaps only their most externally opprobrious vices for the more subtle but no less disappointing ones, there is some room for wondering just how much progress has been made. The continuous and often tiresome plea of authority to critics to remember man's innate humanity and weakness falls on deaf ears when it is made with great unction by men living off the altar, who are so often much quicker to point out the weaknesses of their flock than to admit their own.

The ways of man can be improved. It is the work of the Church to convince men of this. The prime obligation of those doing the work of the Church is to take their personal obligations seriously. Children have little respect for parents who have little respect for their Father, God. Granted that Christ did say that "Physician, cure thyself" was an unfair charge, and that each generation has its own freedom to rebel, leadership is not purely legal responsibility; it is personal responsibility. Nor does sanctity go automatically with the office, as does authority. Every realist admits that somewhere in the area of responsibility lies the great challenge to the Church.

Happily the "big eye" of television and the news media keep very close watch on those charged with authority. The action which cannot be forced from authority by the appeal of the little man to human rights, can be elicited by the fear of public exposure of neglect or malfeasance. Only now are priests and religious breaking into print with their complaints against superiors. Many deplore "washing dirty linen" in public, but far better that it be washed in public than not washed at all. Poverty may be unavoidable but cleanliness is not. In many instances appearing in print has been a last resort to claim the attention of authority. Pressure does get things done; irritating pressure gets them done more quickly.

Education of the masses has also made it more difficult to deceive them. It has given their demands on authority a greater reasonableness, their reactions to authority greater weight, and made revolution superfluous. It has made the responsibility of personal conscience more real in day-to-day living. It has dispensed the Church from making every personal decision for the people, virtually living their lives for them. It has made clearer the mistake of the Church in assuming that her job was to form the consciences of the people rather than to help them form their own consciences.

People who deplore pressures on them and resent the "new" times and "new" things, who see open rebellion in the questioning of authority, are too often influenced by their personal difficulties in living their lives responsibly. If they are subjects they are comfortable as such; they do not want to change their ways. If they are superiors they do not want their orders questioned. No reasonable human being wants more trouble than he can handle. However, the greater difficulties in controlling situations not only save men from tyranny but perhaps assure greater possibility of divine intervention. Regardless of the spiritual implications, the crisis in authority calls for new thoughts, new approaches, and new patterns. And these open out new areas of remarkable development.

Certainly if the Church was ever needed as an influence in the world it is needed today. And if the influence is harder

to exercise it could well be because a better job is being demanded of those wielding authority. This job can be done
if they are willing to give it the time, energy, thought, and
dedication of which they are capable. Those in authority
now are happily much more aware that their jobs are not
sinecures but responsibilities. They realize that there is no
place in the present administrative world for the man who
would live in the past and rest on his laurels. Then, too, if
the job is harder, help is more available. With education so
widespread and leadership so broadly shared, the world is
not so much becoming depersonalized as it is being run by
more and more able people.

Collectively, people generally make wiser decisions than in-
dividually, regardless of their talents. This situation parallels
the marvelously complicated inventions of today which could
never be the work of individuals, but which are the work of
many skillful, inventive men. That the Church should remain the only great organization in the world in which the
say of a single man is all important is almost anachronistic.
And it is so admitted, when the Holy Father has already
approved a synod or senate of bishops to assist him. It is not
that he lacks the authority to do the job, but that he has the
wisdom to refuse the burden of decisions too momentous for
an individual. It is only to be hoped that the senate of bishops
will be selected on the basis of their proven talent rather
than their prestigious positions in their national hierarchies.
It was no accident that brought Vatican II together to declare
the collegiality of episcopal authority. Yet it seems so when
many of those bishops who passed the decree of collegiality
return to their dioceses rejoicing in the sharing of the authority of the pope, without sharing their own authority with their
priests and people. However unhappy they may be about it,
they need only ask themselves if there is any real alternative.
Whatever it may have done in the past, the world today just
will not sit back and wait for the man who cannot make up

his mind, any more than it will tolerate the man whose single thought is law. The man who is deathly afraid of making a mistake and therefore says nothing does not grasp how much more tolerant the world is of honest error than it is of a vacuum.

Seldom has the world looked more hopefully or expectantly to religion and religious leadership than it does today when it is largely confused by its own success, bewildered by the work of its own hands. Nor has that world ever needed more the security coming from acceptance of the fatherhood of God, the realization that He has never really lost control. These, of course, it can get only through religion. But religion can present these only if its leaders are not themselves unduly confused and afraid; if before they give in to the very normal emotional tendency to panic, they realize, as the apostles failed to do, that Christ-God is in the boat with them. What lies before them is not anarchy, but development awaiting direction, crying out for leadership.

The shoemaker's son goes unshod, the doctor refuses to take his own medicine, and the nearer the Church the farther from God are adages simply because history has canonized them. They represent the unfortunate ways of men, their capacity to take what they have for granted and to long only for those things which they have irreparably lost, or can never really have. Yet the world is made livable by those who refuse to be the victims of these clichés of living, by giants who know that charity really begins at home, that you must practice what you preach, that familiarity with holy things need not breed contempt. To be a giant one needs the wisdom of all men, pagans as well as Christians. One needs great knowledge and great courage, and these are not the special prerogatives of the Christian, still too surprised when he sees a virtuous man who does not believe in God. Made as snobbishly exclusive as himself, and believes that the in God's image and likeness, the Christian fancies God to be

Christian alone has priority on virtue. Yet no formal religion in itself profits a man. No man is better for being a member of a special society if he does not have personal integrity. No one is elect because he occupies a high office or belongs to a select group. He must live the life. And this more than anything else is the lesson history would teach us. It is so natural for man to long for the security and peace of heaven, to want to be "saved" before his time, to relax and throw off the tedium of responsibility, to see in moderate prosperity or temporary relief from his burdens a foretaste of heaven, his own election. Yet his Christian destiny is to carry his cross, bear his burden, accept his full responsibilities until God says he is finished, until the task is done. Otherwise he cannot acquire integrity, arrive at his true stature. When Christ pointed out that, because the master was long in coming, the servant began to follow his own inclinations rather than the master's instructions, He clearly outlined the deepest pit before the feet of men. And nowhere is this truer than in the case of churchmen who should be more aware than others of the words of Christ, their validity, their wisdom, and the universality of their application. His words are their business. No one is so impressive as the churchman who acts as though he believes them. They are the words which give him life and make him grow. Christ was no show-off. If by a word He called the dead to life, it was for the explicit purpose of showing men His power to call them to eternal life by His words.

Where history shows the decline of the Church it also shows the words of Christ to have been least effective in the lives of churchmen. Those who will not read history have to learn this the hard way. Perhaps there is no other way for man to learn. But the process is always tragic, the more so when it is unnecessary. Despite his own obvious freedom man has always tended to blame God for the evil around him. The total goodness of God makes this quite unreasonable. The next to get the blame is the Church; and total goodness not being a quality of churchmen, this seems somewhat more reasonable though just as invalid. But the hope for the world is that someday churchmen will really live the Christian life. Then, inspired by their example, man will learn to blame himself for his troubles. He might even decide to do something about them.

G. K. Chesterton is reported to have said that man does not go from bad to worse, he just teeter-totters between puritanical religious legalism and materialistic agnosticism. He is in turn revolted by his own prissiness and piggishness. Certainly all the religious legislation in the world is meaningless if man cannot or will not recognize that morality is only the science of freedom, and that freedom is the basis of all true and lasting love. Love must become in fact, as it has been for two thousand years in theory, the law of the Church. The Church has not so much contented itself with admitting that it has slain the prophets, as it has insisted on making a virtue of having done so. As long as legalism prevails it will continue to be necessary that "one man die for the nation"; and Gamaliel's reasonable plea that "if this is from God it will prevail" will pass unheard. If the fear that freedom will not work is keeping men from giving it a try, one must wonder about the wisdom of God in granting it in the first place. Whatever the case may be, it is equally obvious that the contrary system has not worked, and something else must be found. Freedom is worth a try if for no other reason than that it was God's idea. He must have intended that man reach the zenith of his perfectibility within freedom's framework.

Men dedicated to the development of their own careers within the Church, and receiving the honors and esteem coming with preeminence in the Church, have much to contend with. However, they cannot be dispensed from acquiring the virtue of seeing themselves for what they are and

the great harm they can do the cause of truth by being venal.
It is pitiful to see a man of God rejoicing in a promotion
which he sees as a claim to glory without seeing in it the
heavier obligation to portray the principles of Jesus Christ
by his life. These men above all other men need a knowledge
of history if they would save themselves from being the
actors in a future tragedy.

While no bibliography is given for this book, it must be
noted for those who might wish to read deeper into the episodes of history briefly sketched herein that material for reading is easily available. There is no need to point out sources
of reading for the great East-West schism. Father Grisar's
life of Luther is considered fair by all and there are now
even better ones. *A Pearl to India* and *Wise Man From the
West*, both by Vincent Cronin, are the stories of Roberto de
Nobili and Mateo Ricci. *Thunder in the Distance* by Jacques
Leclercq is the story of Vincent Lebbe, and *Yankee Paul*
by Vincent Holden is the story of Isaac Hecker. These books
are all well researched and authoritative, and leave with the
reader much food for thought.

Chapter 2

Priests and the Priesthood

THE priesthood in any religion has usually been held in high esteem. Whether it has been feared, respected, or actually venerated, it has normally represented status. The priesthood has seldom been held in higher overall esteem than in the Catholic Church of America today. If that esteem has ebbed and flowed at times, been lost or found, it has always been regained when the spirit of Christ has been evident in the priests and the administration of the Church. If it seems to be ebbing at the moment when the Church administration has been compared favorably with the management of General Motors Corporation and the Standard Oil Company of America, it might be because Jesus Christ has become somewhat irrelevant in the management of His Church. Perhaps the comparison is odious, indicative of material prosperity and spiritual poverty in the Church. Perhaps the Church is hoping to be saved more by good management than by the grace of God. Perhaps it has become too legal and not loving enough. Perhaps it has lost its sense of dependence on the Holy Spirit, because the Church seems to be in fairly good hands, with many safeguards and satisfactory legal structures to protect its interests.

It can be argued whether this is really so, but it cannot be questioned that the time has come to make an objective and thoroughly honest appraisal of the Church, its condition, its progress, and its future. This cannot be done without an appraisal of the priests and their work, the reasons underlying their success and failure.

During Vatican II many of the Fathers expressed concern about the image of the Church presented in a press always parched for striking headlines and so eager to pounce on every disagreement about dogma, morals, discipline, or policy. They seemed to fear that the uncomprehending, ever present audience might end up with less respect for the Church and its leaders than would be desirable. This would be a normal reaction in bishops who loved the Church and wanted its leadership presented in the best possible light. They could be forgiven for forgetting the lack of real talent and integrity in every profession and nation in the world. The leadership of the Church would suffer little by comparison with the poor leadership of the world in general. Yet, tending to overrate the antagonism of the world, the Fathers would be too apt to mistake the delight of the spectators at the diversity of the opinions expressed for disillusionment and even scandal, rather than for hope in administrators so obviously sharing their own uncertainties and weaknesses. In the past, people have all too readily and far too often followed leaders who did not know where they were going, and who covered their uncertainty with a lot of noise and ballyhoo. These disillusioned people are more sophisticated now. They are not so easily disappointed because they do not expect so much. But they are looking for leadership by people of greater integrity, more willing to admit they don't know everything, more eager to seek competent help and advice from whatever source it might be available. This is the kind of direction they want from their priests. When they do not get it, there are several reasons for it.

The people of God have not only been permitted and encouraged but, to some degree, even trained to think of their religious leaders as being in direct contact with the unerring divinity. Therefore, to doubt or question them is to doubt or question authority itself. Negatively this has led many people to lose their faith in God, when in reality they have only lost their faith in their leaders. The people have now seen their leaders falter in the face of problems which threaten at all times to get out of hand, and do get terribly out of hand on some occasions. While some of the faithful find themselves very confused at this spectacle, which is a scandal to them, most reasonable people are glad to see that religious leadership no longer makes any pretense of inerrancy in the things of this world. They are relieved to see that their leaders are, like themselves, afraid and uncertain, while remaining honest and courageous. Above all, they do not want the uncertainty of their leaders covered with an air of omniscience or omnipotence, nor these leaders claiming diplomatic immunity from questioning. They do not want their leaders' anxiety for their own glory to keep them from searching out the best answers and listening to the greatest earthly wisdom which they cannot claim as their very own. One expert on the liturgy said that in his work with the committee of bishops preparing the new liturgy, no bishop at any time on any question ever said to him, "What do you think about it?" While the uncertainty and doubt of their leaders can threaten the credulity of the people, it can also restore their faith in the honesty and integrity of men whose claim should not be to inerrancy but to dedication.

There are many people badly shaken in their religious convictions today. However, the pessimists and worrywarts would have a brighter outlook if they could only understand that the world they live in is losing neither its faith nor its hope, but is merely emerging from fantasy into reality which, if anything, is even more religious. It is having fewer and fewer delusions about itself. It is more inclined to look for leadership to those who know their limitations rather than to those who think they know everything. Forty years ago or less, it was common to meet the arrogance of the college man who thought he knew everything. Now only the very young and immature could think so. The extent of education today and the expanded frontiers of accumulated knowledge permit only the consummate fool to think himself omniscient.

So the modern priest must be a different mold of man from his predecessor, who was too often expected not only to take charge but to be right. People need and want his leadership more than ever, but they are also willing to accept his limitations. They expect him to see and accept them too. They want to work with, rather than under him. By these standards the priests in times past have enjoyed unwarranted authority. People followed the collar rather than the man, the uniform rather than the person. In these times of admitted trial the Church can no longer expect to create leaders by appointment but must seek out those qualified for leadership. Not only must leaders be sought among the priests, but the material for the priesthood must be sought among the leaders. Contrary to expectation and hope, the appointment of a man to a position of power does not endow him with the ability he needs for the job. So the man with the talent for the job must be sought out and appointed to the job. The willingness to do this will represent a very radical change of thought pattern in the Church. Very little vision or judgment is required to see that extreme urgency exists here. Not only must no talent be rejected, but every possible talent must be found and exploited. When one considers the elaborate scouting systems for producing the athletic material demanded in the field of professional sport, one wonders what might be the end results of such a system employed in the production of apostles. The vast scouting systems of the industrial giants of America scouring the universities for all possible talent are indeed worthy of imitation.

Regardless of the invaluable lay help available to authority now, and even more so in the near future, leadership for at least a generation in the Church is going to be found mainly in the priesthood. It is all the more important therefore to understand the priests, what they are and how they got that way. The changes which are demanded by the priesthood of the future will have to be explored if the priesthood is to be ready, able, and willing for the tasks which will always remain the tasks of the priesthood.

There are some negative but very consequential observations to be made about attitudes toward priests and the priesthood. These have colored the thinking of the people of God. They have made criticism of either the institution or the men in it difficult, if not impossible, without scandalizing the faithful or incurring the wrath of authority. Yet never has the Church or the priesthood so needed the intelligent and goodwilled criticism of thoughtful people.

There is a familiar expression which gives a clue to the serious misunderstanding of priests. That expression is *alter Christus* — another Christ. There can be little doubt about the sincerity of those who use this expression to describe the priest, for he should surely be, above all, Christlike. But the term tends to encourage the attributing to the priest of qualities he simply does not have. And unfortunately the priest is often much too willing to accept the attribution. If, from one special point of view, the role of a priest makes him another Christ, so does the role of the layman, who also must pick up his cross and follow Christ, make him Christlike. But to the priest is reserved the title, and so also the delusion. This can lead the priest to accept the title without feeling the comparable obligation to live the Christlike life.

Eagerness to believe exposes anyone to credulity and superstition. Thus the eager Christian is exposed to an effect something like the effect of Communist brainwashing. He

is apt to lose his objectivity. And this danger is very real for
the priests who come from homes in which the priest has
been deeply respected and criticism of him severely suppressed.
When young men go from these homes to seminaries where
they are taught that the priest should be this and that,
and specific ideals held up to them, they are very apt to be
victims of a tragic mistake. When they one day attain
their cherished goal, they may assume that they have also
reached the ideal. Whether the lavishness of the ordination
ceremony, the external celebration of the occasion, or the
exaltation which comes from arrival at the long-awaited goal
is the main factor in the delusion, the delusion is there.
Any goal such as the priesthood, for which a real man is willing to forgo something as basic as sexual pleasure and the
innate desire to reproduce himself, can surely expose one to
delusions of grandeur. Nor should it ever be forgotten that
this willingness is the basic reason for the high esteem of
the people for their priests. Very earnest thought and effort
must go into assuring that such delusion does not happen.
When ideals are pointed out, reason must work validly
around them, leaving no room for delusion.

Priests are allowed or encouraged or anxious to forget that
they remain fully human beings. Perfection is made the goal
of those who cannot be perfect; incorruptibility is made the
ideal of those who are corruptible; adequate and unfailing
strength is attributed to those who are weak. When these
people are made by real life and living to face their humanity
squarely, they are confused. The necessary compromise with
their humanity often leads to the unnecessary compromise
of their principles. They realize too late that they have been
leading their people to the phony *alter Christus* rather than
to the *Christus*; they have undertaken a human success story
rather than a divine one. Like so many people today they
have been too influenced by the movie presentation of the
hero-priest.

Priests, like other people, have personal problems, yet this very idea seems incongruous to the average person. If it is incongruous it is because the people have been encouraged to believe that priests are above such problems. The faults and failings of priests have been hushed up or glossed over. The priests have lived so far apart from their people that their faults were not apparent, perhaps indeed so that they would not be apparent. And because their faults are not obvious to the people, many priests have subconsciously assumed that their failings do not really matter. The inference is that it does not matter what the priest really is, provided that he faithfully gives the public service that is publicly expected of him. A good look at the facts would clearly indicate that a priest can only give what is expected of him if he is what he ought to be. And he can never be that unless he knows what he is and is willing to see himself as he is. Then he will not only allow God to make something of him, but will beg Him to do so. Even spiritual men seldom realize the resistance they offer the work of God in their souls. This resistance comes mainly from their willingness and even anxiety to believe they are already good enough. The constant stressing of ideals rather than the honest acceptance of themselves as "unprofitable servants" encourages this mentality.

Priestly character can be developed if the priest first of all knows himself, and then the ideal to which he aspires. However, the humanity he shares with the politician makes him overanxious to cover himself with the mantle of his office. Eager as he may be at the altar offering the sacrifice of Christ to take on the identity of Christ, he must never lose sight of his own identity. (Fewer priests would be eager to be bishops if they realized how far above them was the priesthood itself). The *alter Christus* figure of speech has been greatly overworked. In their training, the priests-to-be have come to know more about Christ than they learned about themselves.

Too many priests are also victims of the teaching that they are first, last, and always "the priest." However praiseworthy this may be in urging the priest to live a life worthy of the cause he represents, it contains the inherent and extreme danger of letting him forget that he is first of all a person, then a man, and last of all a priest. Too often the implication has been that if the man is a good priest he is a good man. Yet if the priest is not basically a real person he can hardly be a real priest. If he is not a real man he is hardly qualified for the priesthood, which, at least until now, has been reserved for males, if not always for men.

Equating the job with the man has created the tendency to think of the priest as a functionary rather than as a human being with his own identity apart from the priesthood. This has led to his being considered a part of a machine. He can easily become a nameless, faceless cog in the machinery of the Church, incapable of his own opinions, dedicated completely and entirely to the Church's dogma and policies, as if his functions did not involve personal conviction or commitment. When the priest is satisfied in such a role, and there can be no doubt he has been encouraged to be so, he justifies the charge that the Church practices the total tyranny it condemns. That the individual exists only for the good of the whole is often substantiated by the Church's use and handling of its priests, despite its condemnation of the teaching. Regardless of the motive, the priest until now has existed only for the good of the Church and its people. His own personal destiny has been secondary. What has made this inevitable, pardonable, and even understandable is that this lack of consideration for the priest as a person has come from his assumed dedication to the ideal, his assumed willingness to sacrifice all for the flock. The assumption is not valid.

It is the tradition of the sea that the captain go down with the ship, or at least be the last man off the ship. Unless the captain is a hero he will fail in this challenge, or meet it either because of respect of persons or his inability to avoid it. This is at best pseudoheroism, a much more frequent thing than heroism. It is not virtue. The priest in fact has seldom been challenged to practice virtue. Strange as it seems, he has seldom been taught what real virtue is or how it is acquired. It is usually assumed that he has it because he is a priest, much as it is assumed that a soldier is brave because he is a soldier and has never been caught running away from the enemy. A priest cannot be made holy by ordination; he must acquire holiness, like any other virtue, through practice. Willing submission to rules and regulations does not make a man of virtue any more than the regime of convicts in a penitentiary makes men of good habits and principles. Conformity has only a mechanical similarity to the freely formed habits which constitute virtue. Needless to say, the priest carries the effects of this training into his life. These do not make him what he is, but they shape him to an appreciable degree. The assumption that he has acquired virtue when he has only conformed is largely responsible for a way of thinking in the priesthood which has led to many defects in the priest's work. These defects are not helping him to meet the challenge of the modern day when many would have the executive replace the apostle. And if they are not recognized, understood, and eliminated, religion will have become business, efficiency will have replaced zeal, and buildings, rather than charity, will characterize the overall picture.

When one mistake is made, error easily follows error. The priest, having the ideal held up to him throughout his training, too easily assumes that when he reaches the position he reaches the ideal, or so reasonably close that he need only allow for the human factor. Naturally that human factor is much greater than he allows for. He gradually comes to accept that if he sees nothing wrong with himself or his fellow priests, there is nothing wrong with them. Considering the normal man's penchant for self-deceit, wishful thinking, and escape from reality, delusion is very close at hand. Yet despite the professed love of truth, there has been a very notable reticence in the Church, and among religious people, about seeing the defects of the machine and therefore the defects of the people whose work the Church is. This blindness has been excused and even promoted under the guise of charity or loyalty to Christ; but it has been made inescapable by the nearly universal rejection of honest criticism. It has been sanctified by invoking the sacred cow of respect for authority. This turnabout is something to wonder at in a religion which has canonized examination of the individual conscience, while virtually dispensing authority from accountability, as if there were no higher authority. Few people can understand the degree to which the acceptance of every whim of incompetents and phonies has been made a virtue in the Church. This "virtue" has led to the disarming of the good priest and the neutralization of the apostle. Those who would deny this either repudiate history or interpret it to suit themselves. But it has happened only because of the senseless efforts of men to hide their humanity from themselves. This "virtue" explains the desperate effort of authority to clothe itself in divinity. It indicates that churchmen have forgotten that God has chosen to use them, however poor and frail instruments they are. They were not meant to use Him to cover their frailty. Through their weakness God was to show His strength. Covering their weakness with His strength would make weakness a virtue.

Any virtue pushed to excess becomes a vice. Obedience became the great post-Reformation virtue. All priests were urged to be good, to be humble, and above all to be obedient. Countless spiritual writers pointed to disobedience as the very stuff of pride, the root of all evil. Thus the "good" priest in his honest effort to avoid disobedience, cost what it may, has become quite obsequious. This was what created the "scandal" of the progressives at Vatican II who dared to question not only the deeds but the very motives of those in authority. It was the equating of obsequiousness with obedience which made it seem impossible for a man in authority to be bad or dishonest, and nearly as impossible for a subject to be honest and dedicated without being obsequious. Certainly a subject could never be considered as dedicated to Christ, God, and truth as is a superior. This subtle thought process crept in through the best motives of fine men, eager to do everything to insure the best conduct of the Church. But because it became an extreme measure, it departed from the middle road of virtue and brought disaster. Obedience became the source of virtue rather than the foundation of it. Docility became the witness of grace in the soul; conformity became the evidence of sanctity. But when conformity is identified with obedience, God has been made to serve man, and God's grace becomes man's private currency.

There have been many unfortunate effects of the carry-over of monastic spiritual formation into priestly formation. One of them has come from the canonization of silence. Silence was made a virtue, and the penalty being paid for this mistake is the present dearth of ideas coming from people dedicated to God, people who should have ideas and voice them. Silence was recommended as an aid to recollection. But silence soon became commendable in itself even when it signified an intellectual vacuum. While many garrulous people show by their speech how vacuous they are, many others have nothing to say because they are thoughtless. The quiet man may be thoughtful but not necessarily because of his silence. It may be a means to an end but it certainly is not an end in itself. Music makes that abundantly clear. Silence in itself is sterile. Who can doubt the sterility of most religious silence? Many religious use it as a glorious escape from the unpleasant truth or from endless prattling about trivia, the general recreational diet of people who look upon discussion of deeper and better things as either pedantry or unwarranted distraction.

Silence has often represented a dispensation from thought

when it has not meant a prohibition of it. So the Church has
been deprived of the fruit of many of its best minds, its best
ideas. To some degree silence has buried the talents of the
best endowed intellects in the Church. Those who deny this
point with pride to many brilliant minds who are the orna-
ments of the Church, but those who affirm it can point with
deep and sincere regret to the very few glorious minds the
Church produced considering the long custodianship of learning it has had through many ages. Considering the centuries-
long monopoly of the Church on education there is a scarcity
of great work in proportion to the number of men who made
a voluntary offering of all they had to God. Because of the
monastic formation of the clergy in which silence was so
sacrosanct, the go-getter, the zealous productive priest, has
been suspect. The docile conformist, the quiet one, has been
a consolation to his superiors, a reliable person, easy to handle.
This attitude has impoverished the Church. To it more than
anything else can be attributed the present dearth of religious
leadership.

In the current confusion occasioned by the new things in
the Church, one thing is becoming increasingly evident in relation to monastic or religious silence. It has allowed large
numbers of emotional cripples and withdrawn personalities
to escape early detection, treatment, and possibly a cure.
These new things are forcing many religious to face the demands of charity and the apostolate. Whereas the quiet retir-
ing religious was highly approved, now the outgoing, loving,
involved person is not only in high demand, but apparently
in low supply. The quiet religious found in silence the shield
he sought against rejection and hurt, real and imaginary. Now
with this silence all but gone, his true state is quite obvious,
as is the reason that it escaped detection.

The role of humility is basic in the Christian, and more so
in the priest. Where there is no humility there is no virtue.
However, the monastic trend has been to avoid pride rather

than to acquire humility. Thus superiors have tended far more to monitor and even suppress the talents of subjects than to seek out proper investment of them for their growth and development. It has been too easy for superiors to confuse their honest efforts to safeguard the humility of their subjects with their envy of a better endowed subject who must be kept in his place. Thus they have tended to be overcautious stewards, more interested in their own image and in avoiding personal losses than in developing an efficient corps of highly qualified servants for the people of God. Let there be no mistake. The most venal and vain can be those who insist on leaving a heritage behind. But usually their heritage consists of what trivial evidence there is of their own passage through time. Once our great institutions were called after saints for obvious reasons. Then it became acceptable to call them after the more notable churchmen who were quite properly deceased. Now the country is pockmarked with institutions named after the very living men who ordered their construction and who seem strangely unaware of Christ's admonition not to let the left hand know what the right is doing. It is fantastic that men of God can build their own monuments and look in the face the people whose alms actually erected and paid for them. The heritage which should be, but seldom is, left is the careful searching out and fruitful use of all the talent and zeal of both priest and layman in the development of the people of God in goodness.

No reasonable bishop could doubt that he has several priests in his diocese with much greater talent than himself. Yet it is almost universally accepted that the bishop has to be the knight in shining armor who slays all the dragons. The Catholic press is dedicated to his heroic image, and God help the man who doubts it. This is a human quality not restricted to the Church, but the fact remains that some spirituality or love of God should make the bishop as aware of this as others are. The bishop's position carries a double obligation to utilize

all the human talent available to him for the honor and glory
of God. He should have at least as much fear of pride, ambition, and self-seeking in himself as he has in his subjects. But
as yet, the bishops have to be chosen from among the priests.
And they are still burdened with a spirituality erroneously
implying some mysterious grant of supplementary talent and
assurance against error on appointment to authority. This is
a hard conviction to escape even for men with enough honesty
to realize that they did not have the talent for the job before
the appointment. It would seem such a small step for them
to understand that God does supply, not with some miraculous
personal endowment, but with the availability of many
talented people who too often pass unnoticed because of the
blind pride of those who will not see. The divine help is
sought within rather than without where it is so often available
in lavish supply. If a bishop has this tragic pride, he did not
acquire it as a bishop; he had it as a priest. If such pride is one
of the qualifications for a bishop, then many priests are indeed
qualified. Many priests resent anything their bishop tells them.
If he indicates what is to be done he is running the diocese
by himself; if he leaves them on their own he has no interest,
shows no leadership.

Few priests are so fortunate as to have their good qualities
and talents developed by accident. Yet, from being nothing
the day before ordination to becoming a fully finished product
the day after ordination is the pattern in the priesthood.
From the day of ordination, the young priest gets little of the
training and help that young men in other professions receive
on beginning their careers. By ordination the young priest has
reached (until now at least) an irreversible point in his life.
Two things can happen. Either the young man himself simply
cannot be told anything, or those around him cannot, or will
not, tell him anything. There is no internship, no system of
postgraduate training for him. Even he assumes erroneously
that he comes from the seminary fully trained. Little or no

discrimination is exercised in placing young priests under men of stature who are interested in bringing out the best in the young man, helpful to him on his way toward success in handling the business of the Church. The task of preparing young priests for the work of spiritual direction, qualifying them as competent guides and counselors, aiding them in the transition from the seminary seclusion to real involvement through availability to their people, has hardly been efficaciously explored. The changes being made in seminary curricula and horaria only confuse inevitability and desperation with planning and vision.

Will change for the sake of change accomplish anything? Is it not a case of novelty creating an atmosphere which will disappear when the novelty has worn off? Surely the basic idea of Christianity is to change the heart of the individual, and there is little good or bad about change or stability except in reference to that essential. Therefore the fundamental problem in the priesthood is the fundamental human problem, pride. The monastic approach to pride was called the "Chapter of Faults." The origin and basis for this act of religion was the calculated progress in virtue purportedly coming from such an act. The public accusation of self and/or others was to enable the accuser as well as the accused to face himself, correct and improve his performance for the love of God. However, this exercise depended on the readiness and willingness of the individual, which could not be forced nor made present by the ringing of a bell at a specific time. So personal pride was not faced nor was virtue automatically inculcated. Most realists want the whole exercise thrown out as something ridiculous, but it has been canonized by time, even though like many other traditions it has little but time to recommend it. Because it is old, it is considered, like old wine, to be good. Time also makes corruption more corrupt.

The trouble with the Chapter of Faults was that it became a formality. Whether it involved the accusation of self or others, it involved concentration on self and others to a very unprofitable degree and in a very unprofitable way, a way which could hardly be called Christian. Since nothing of a serious moral nature could be used, it tended to enhance trivia, leading to the straining out of the gnat and the swallowing of the camel. That it was not intended to do so mattered little in the result. It had much the same effect as the canonization of the phrase, "doing the ordinary things extraordinarily well." A few overemphasized the importance of the ordinary things, making mountains out of molehills, and most did not even do the ordinary things well. However, the Chapter of Faults failed in the acid test. It did not make correction a more acceptable thing. Religious remained as resentful as other people of correction, indicating a proportionately greater pride in consideration of their religious profession. Too many human devices calculated to be aids to virtue rebound and tie good men up in themselves, leading them to pursue virtue more for the prestige that it brings, and its influence on men, than for the love of God. However praiseworthy these devices or the motives of the men who originated them, they have not added much to the formula of Jesus Christ for holiness: that a man should love God with his whole heart, and his neighbor as himself, for the love of God. Coming from the Son of God this seems a fairly final definition. It seems silly to try to improve on it. Holiness seems assured when Jesus Christ really matters to the priest. His Chapter of Faults is more productive when he gets it as it comes through the public press, the candid criticism of his flock, the interested observations of his superiors, and the inevitable frustrations of personal pride in dealing with the very people who need him most. The greatest problem of any priest is his personal pride; his willingness to handle it is in proportion to his love of God.

The apostolate is essential to the priesthood. It is very difficult to see how a priest can sanctify himself by withdrawing from the world which Christ, the priest, came to save. The eremitical life is justified only by its part in the salvation of souls. The apostolate means involvement with people. Yet separation from the people has been made a virtue in the priesthood. The seminary course until now has been largely the negative discipline of conformity, rather than the positive development of those qualities needed by a priest, not only for his survival but to exercise his special influence in the world. After ordination numerous if senseless diocesan statutes are invoked to keep him good and untouched by the world. A full-grown man is told that he must be in by eleven o'clock at night, when he should have been trained to be responsible. Young men, after being imprisoned in a seminary and laid to rest each night by the bell, rebel against this. Instead of learning, as any normal human being does, that he cannot stay up all night and do his work the next day, he simply refuses to keep good hours because he has kept them for too long against his will. Going to bed when it suits him is a manifestation of his liberation, whereas going to bed when he ought to should be a manifestation of his interest in his work. The tendency of the young priest to revel in his liberty is quite marked. In the apostolate, the tendency is to become involved with the people he likes rather than with those who need him. If this attitude continues too long the young priest finds himself so far removed from his original intention and purpose that he is damaged beyond repair. If he is really fortunate he may be awakened, sadder if not wiser, by some jolting personal experience. The Church has in any case virtually lost its greatest asset, a real priest.

It is not sufficient to say that seminary training is changing, or that the young man entering the seminary today simply will not conform, so that such factors will be automatically eliminated. Whatever any system of seminary training has to offer, it has its own built-in defects. It cannot, *per se*, touch the man being trained. The priestly vocation, of its nature, demands involvement with people and the involvement is one of love. Where there is no love there is no involvement, nor is there any such thing as being a good priest apart from people. They are the very stuff of priestly work. This involvement cannot be legislated; it is the firstfruit of the love of God. It can be inspired by zealous priest friends, by helpful and exemplary pastors, by bishops who are first of all shepherds rather than business administrators. But if and when it deepens and grows, it does so almost entirely through the grace of pastoral rewards realized from the deep love and respect of people honestly served and lovingly aided in their religious and personal needs. Under God, the bishop can be most helpful in this regard.

It may be noted in the questionnaire in the appendix that a large percentage of the priests believe their bishops are quite accessible to them. However, it should be noted that the priests who answered it are mostly pastors of upper middle years and therefore of some prominence and importance in their dioceses. Most of these priests do not need or want to see much of their bishops. And when they do want to see them the bishops are usually available. But it is the younger priests who need accessibility to the bishop. In reality they have the least of it. While he ordained them as a father, he has often virtually disowned them. When they need him most he is not available; when he sends for them it is often too late to change the course of events. Some early and real interest in the young priest would do more good than two hours of remonstrance when it is too late. The young priest usually remains quite unimpressed by an upbraiding of the bishop; he would be quite impressed by real interest in his welfare.

There is, thank God, a greater willingness now than ever to face the fact of problem priests. Some practical things on a minor scale are being done for them. Although some progress was inevitable, few question that more is being done because of the wider attention to the matter in the public press. However, it makes one wonder when civic organizations and lay groups have been faster to see and understand the problems than have the clergy supposedly motivated by greater charity.

There is little accommodation of the young priest's talents to his job. Those assigning the young men hardly know them, and in large dioceses certainly do not know them. The young priest is expected to be so pliable in the hands of his superiors that it is of no consequence where he is to be sent or what he is to do, or what his qualifications may be for the task to which he is assigned. He is seldom consulted or given an opportunity to express his inclinations. Then, of course, he is supposed to have abrogated all his human rights. He is treated like a child when others his age are being respectfully heard by superiors eager for whatever contribution can be made to the progress of industry or civic enterprise or political development. In large dioceses he is too old when he comes to the time for an appointment to responsibility. His best years have been wasted in conforming to chores moderated by the indifferent. When his people really need him most, his appointment to a parish is a benefice, to some degree a sinecure.

The toll is very high. But again it must be said that these things are being talked about everywhere, and there is growing pressure for action. But why should that action be forced by circumstances or by a virtual revolution, when charity should have assured it? What is being done is too little and too slow. Many fear that by the time the action is taken, the need for it will have ceased to be, for there will be too few young priests. And while it is true that quick decisions and developments are not necessarily good ones, and that few priests object to necessary delays, almost all object to the delays due to ineptitude, disinterest, and poor organization. There are many priests of high executive ability available. Surely the Church must not permit, in this day of admitted urgency, disastrous and unnecessary delay because an individual superior cannot be disturbed by reason of old age or ill health.

Nothing takes a heavier toll of priests than does chastity. Few doubt the urgency called for in attending to this matter. Nor is all the anxiety of the young priest, to say nothing of the young candidate for the priesthood, for the abandonment of celibacy, but rather for attentive study and decision on the matter. Most priests are amazed, if not shocked, to see the amount of space given in the public press to the matter of priestly celibacy. This attention seems merely to point up one of the unfortunate facts of Catholic life — that little is going to be done by the Church until and unless enough publicity is given the question to embarrass those in authority to the point of action. It is a truism to say that the squeaking wheel gets the grease, the importuner has the door opened to him. The Church has not, and without heavy pressures will not, set up structures and procedures for expeditiously handling the rights and wrongs involved in progress. The basic cause of this is twofold. First, the Church lives in the fog of traditionalism. Second, although infallibility has pertained primarily to the popes and the councils, there is that fatal aura of infallibility about every bishop and the officials of his chancery which makes avoiding normal mistakes a fetish. The thought of making a mistake, and above all a public one, is a trauma to little men who just have to be right even when they know they cannot always be so. It is this fetish which produces the ludicrous picture of a whole diocese standing around waiting for an answer that many a child would be competent to give without delay, or brings the embarrassing "no comment" from men who should really know what to say.

Not only the people of God, but even the bishop and superior, delight in the fine young priest, highly competent and qualified, willing to be told at a moment's notice what is wanted of him and where he is to go. He is a gem. And if he can stand the demands made upon him because of what he is, he will be an ornament to the Church, a joy to his superiors, and, most important of all, a happy man. If he cannot stand the pace he will either have a physical, emotional, or mental breakdown, or become bitter. If not embittered, it might well be because he has taken the same course as many others before him, talented but tired out. He may relinquish his goal of happiness and settle for mere pleasure.

Since the day that Judas made up his twisted mind to take the thirty pieces of silver and get off the sinking ship, priests have turned their backs on what they have considered to be their calling, their life's work. There is no need to gloss over their doing so, explain it away, deny it, or cover it up. Christ was sorry for the betrayal of Judas, sorry for Judas, but He was not apologetic for having chosen him, or ashamed of having called him. He accepted the fact of Judas' free choice to do wrong. Priests today still have that free choice and exercise it. It is a tribute to the high public opinion of priests that when they do make use of this freedom to abandon the priesthood it makes the world press.

When priests do wrong the reasons are fairly basic. Every human being needs to be loved more than any other thing in life. Love is more precious to most than the air they breathe. So many would rather die than live unloved. The priest is no exception. And he is just as prone as his neighbor to forget that it is hard to love someone who is just not lovable and will not make much effort to be so. Yet it remains a fact that in the religion which made a virtue of love — and love is the only law of the New Testament — the training of priests has tended to make a virtue of not loving, of not being involved. Their training has implied that any relationship with a woman which is slightly more than casual is an occasion of sin. They are sent to a ministry in which a great deal of their work will be with women, with the weird conviction that knowing almost nothing about them can have some mysterious advantage. Apart from the fact that much of the general advice on chastity given to young priests in times past was all but utterly ridiculous, their ignorance of what was involved in taking and living the vow of chastity was monumental.

Chastity, in the post-Reformation nightmare and through Victorian puritanism, became the virtue which eliminated sex rather than regulated love. Only now is it generally realized that a loveless life is an unhappy life, that the failure to love is a failure in one of the two essentially human functions. Man is distinguished from the brute in his ability to think and his capacity to love. No one lacking either of these is fully human. Man simply cannot be dispensed from his God-given onus to both learn and love. That does not mean that he has to have a sexually active life, but it does mean that he cannot have a loveless life, which far too many people do have. Only a love-filled life can make a sexless life happy. The man who is technically chaste without loving fills his life with things rather than people. These, like sex alone, can give a man pleasure but they cannot give him happiness. Only love can do that. It can do it with sex for those entitled to sex, and without sex for those who have given up sex for reasons of love.

The open acknowledgment that chastity without love has been a failure has made celibacy material for restudy and appraisal in depth. Many insist that the vow of chastity be eliminated, or at least made voluntary or arbitrary for candidates to the priesthood. But the great argument for voluntary celibacy is not voided because one must be a celibate to be a priest in the western Church. Celibacy, like any other freely chosen obligation, is voluntary. A man is not less voluntarily married because he has assumed marital obligations. Those who would reject this voluntariness simply want the priesthood and all that goes with it except the celibacy. They would have the loving privileges of marriage without its obligations.

There is something selfish and immature about this. Their complaint about celibacy is not so much that it is not voluntary as that it is irrescindable.

All agree that there should never be a time when a son of the Church wanting readmission to the body of the faithful should be refused. And this should include priests who have fallen away and sought the solaces of a wife and family. But they did freely seek the priesthood knowing that celibacy went with it. It has been charged that many did not fully understand what they were doing, and this charge alone is sufficient for a thorough restudy of the whole question, which should not be long delayed. However, there should be no question of scrapping the vow, especially in this day of the "sexual revolution" when a celibate life by real people is needed as it was never needed before. The day that the priest cannot be celibate it must be admitted that married people cannot remain faithful, chaste. This is an admission of the spiritual bankruptcy of the people of God. The Christian religion cannot be bankrupt. Christians can be, but never God. Nowhere is the strength of the Church more clearly visible than in celibacy. While celibacy is asking far too much of anyone who does not know what it is all about, and it is demanding too much of anyone not adequately prepared for such a life, a difficult job is not an impossible one. Celibacy does call for adequate preparation, dedication, and hard work at holiness.

Whatever else is said, it cannot be denied that Christ was celibate. And while He can be pointed out as having a divine nature as well as a human one, He did recommend the life of celibacy and make it possible by His grace. That some should fail to rise to the heights to which they aspired should not be surprising, but this is not to say that the heights are not there to be scaled. Few have ever undertaken anything in life without failure at some time or to some degree. Nor is perfection in chastity any more demanding than perfection in any other virtue, or than perfection itself. The state of chastity and the willingness of normal human beings to embrace it for the sake of Christ and the kingdom of God on earth are among the great weapons in man's fight against the domination of whimsy and self-indulgence. Certainly the road of chastity was never intended to be an easy one, nor was celibacy indiscriminately recommended, but it was to be walked by many whose discrimination would lead them to choose it.

Celibacy is a fact of the Christian way of life, and as such it has worked moderately well. Imposed on the clergy in a time and age when it certainly did not work any better than it does today, and was not more acceptable, it should not be hastily abandoned. But its restudy is mandatory, and no number of exhortations or decrees will make it otherwise. The delay in the restudy, just because it is unnecessary, will only bring those recommending its abandonment closer to the day of their dreams, and those supporting it closer to the day of their dreads. However one may look at it, a mature restudy can do nothing but good to the Church. But the most learned and articulate representatives of both sides must be heard, and their arguments studied. It is my conviction that while celibacy should not be separated from the priesthood, the priesthood which demands celibacy should definitely be separated from many things to which it has, through custom, been tied. The greatest care must be taken to understand that celibacy was not a *conditio sine qua non* of ordination. Nor is marriage in itself any insurmountable obstacle to the priesthood. The two ways of life are not in themselves conflicting. There is no reason why there should not be exceptions, as there are to every rule. The Church should never allow itself to become priest-ridden. But before exaggerated fears of the shortage of priests dictate emergency measures which might be regretted and irremediable, let the vast areas of Church administration, now the preserves of the clergy, be opened to the laity. Let the possibility of married religious be considered today, when the adult layman has so many competencies desperately required by the Church to meet growing demands in fields which in no way require priestly orders. Whole areas of apostolic work should be explored and turned over to the laity, single and married. Seventy percent of all the foreign mission work could be done by them. Doing this would perhaps put the attack on celibacy in better perspective because the priesthood demanding celibacy would no longer be necessary for these fields. In other words, before jettisoning a strictly celibate priesthood, which would mean an incalculable loss to the Church, let the many alternatives be studied in great detail with high competence. They probably contain not only the answer to this problem but also the key to the expansive work of the Church in a contracting world in desperate need of its guidance and influence.

To me, the present-day cry for a priesthood with optional celibacy represents retrogression, a retreat from a position of the Church in the world which, despite recognized defects, has great meaning for the world. When a sufficient number of young men are not found to give up all things including marriage for Christ and His work, not God but the Church is dead. Individual Christians must become more and more like Christ. Christ was celibate. Young men will be found to accept this challenge. The Christian way of life is not retrogressive any more than is the evolutionary process. If vocations are scarce, and it depends on how the matter is considered, might it not be because there have been too many religious and priests and not enough good ones? Could it not be that badly fulfilled ministries, rather than unrealistic demands made in the name of celibacy, have led to the reputed scarcity of priests? An uninspiring clergy can never stimulate vocations. Could the apparent shortage of priests be a challenge to the Church to find a more realistic solution to the problem than the frantic, panic-stricken prayers for more people to dedicate themselves to a way of life which is being directed and handled rather badly? It would seem so. The bitter reaction of most priests to criticism of their personal lives, which all too little resemble that of Christ, would support such a theory. Wrong criticism inflicts a minor wound, but correct criticism cuts to the bone and brings a bitter reaction. Priests generally have not wanted to hear it. But if the Church is brought sufficiently low they will have to hear it, and then they will know that celibacy has not been the problem but the answer. Who honestly doubts that where the Church has been and is highly respected it is primarily because of celibacy vowed and kept? Celibacy represents the victory of grace over nature. It testifies far more broadly and effectively to the supernatural than do all the shrines and miracles in the world. Where celibacy has been practiced faithfully the Church has prospered. Where it existed in name only, mocking reality, it languished and all but died.

The honest man knows that celibacy is best for the priest. Christ recommended it. Few doctors would doubt that if the best service and care of the sick were the end of medicine as practiced, celibacy would be best for medical men, too, however impracticable it might be otherwise. In the apostolate of the Church the care of the flock is the essential obligation of the priest, and he knows that this is so. Celibacy is, by far, the most desirable state for men doing this work. But what must and can be questioned is whether so many should be priests, whether many who are priests should have been, and whether a man who has become bitter about a commitment he has made for life should be compelled to persist in it.

By implying that a forced retreat from celibacy for the clergy of the western Church is retrogression, I do not mean to imply that the present laws of celibacy are necessarily the best, or even adequate. Everything can be improved. Nor do I mean to imply that marriage renders one inferior to the celibate. Surely there is far too much evidence that superior people, married or celibate, will show themselves superior in whatever they do. Celibacy in itself can no more assure the spiritual growth and development of the Christian than marriage of necessity impedes it. Celibacy is always going to appear shoddy and ineffectual when men of inferior caliber or materialistic orientation are permitted to undertake the celibate life in the name of God. Christian marriage appears equally shoddy when married people are more interested in the event of the marriage than the qualifications for the Christian life in marriage. When a celibate clergy is performing so inadequately that celibacy itself is debatable, many other areas should be investigated before celibacy itself is questioned. When the deviations of a celibate clergy are more glaring than their ministrations are impressive, many questions must indeed be asked. But surely the questions should start with the quality of the celibates as people, their training and their work, rather than with the state of celibacy. For who actually believes a priest is less effective, all other things being equal, because of celibacy? The fact is that we are being exposed to a great number of pleas for a change in the laws of celibacy before the question of the training and work of celibates has been discussed in depth.

Although things are belatedly improving, the preparation of candidates for the celibate life has been not so much inadequate as hopeless. Sex thoughts have generally by implication been construed as evil thoughts, when no sane man could responsibly take a vow of chastity without thinking about sex very deeply and thoroughly. Although the Catholic Church is again belatedly insisting on sex education in the schools, sex education has been virtually forbidden to religious. Many religious honestly set about counseling the young without themselves having any real knowledge of sex, despite the importance of this element in the development of the young. It was insisted that parents were the ones to teach sex to their children. But the truth of the matter was that parents generally had not the knowledge, the vocabulary, or the articulateness to do this job.

The inadequacy of the sexual instruction of candidates for the priesthood has been due to two factors. The first is the scholastic tendency to fragment the human personality, much as a doctor would separate the heart from the body and treat it as if it were an independent entity. Man's home life, economic life, social life, civic life, academic life, love life are not separate lives, but phases of one integral life. The spiritual life of a man has been given undue emphasis, not because it is undeserving of emphasis, but as if it could be developed apart from the rest. This has led to a pseudospirituality in pious people who actually lack personal wholeness. A man's spiritual life is only one aspect of his integral life as a human being. He grows and develops as a human being, not as a disembodied spirit. The path to holiness is strewn with the emotional wrecks of people who thought that becoming holy meant the denial of their humanity. The number of religious women who have been taught implicitly or explicitly that the love of any human being, male or female, militated against their love of God and fidelity to Him, is legion. And this despite the fact that St. John so clearly states, "If a man does not love his neighbor whom he sees, how can he love God whom he sees not?" Christ said that a man must love God with his whole heart, and his neighbor too. Obviously Christ did not think that love of neighbor took away from the love of God. The fact is that people vowing their lives to chastity were led to believe that they were obligated to some kind of love other than human, a love which had no sexual content, which was purely spiritual — in other words, quite beyond them. How can a reasonable human being deny his humanity without repudiating the creation of almighty God? Yet what priest has not done this to some degree in his honest effort to be a good priest? Being good is the zenith of human endeavor, and so it is difficult. But it has been made impossible by approaching the task unrealistically. This lack of realism is one of the basic deterrents to young people who might otherwise undertake a life which is rewarding in the very thing which many would exclude from the celibate life, in loving. Lack of realism has obliterated the Christian teaching that a man does not go to heaven for *being* good, but for the persevering effort to be good, for the efficacious desire to be better than he is.

The second factor involved in the inadequacy of training for celibacy is the element of human pride. Rightly ashamed of much of its history and the conduct of many of its members, the Church has made a great effort to atone. It has prided itself on the fact of the reforms after the Council of Trent, reforms provoked by the conditions which led to the Reformation. But like all organizations intent on reform, which fail to see that the goal is far more apt to be the approval of the world than the approval of God, to remove the shame rather than to atone for the sin, the Church has rejoiced too quickly in the dehumanizing of its religious. Gifts, talents, and graces have become dangerous things to be hidden, not used. The good-looking priest of charm and zeal is suspect, for his own protection of course. Anonymity has been made a virtue to safeguard humility, except in the case of authority when publicity has effected good public relations. Personal endowments of associates are boasted of publicly but censured privately. The jealousy of the less endowed is presented as reasonable solicitude for the good of the gifted.

The Church has reformed for the love of God but the people of God have become proud of themselves for doing it. The Church has become somewhat obnoxious, like the reformed drunk so proud of his success and so contemptuous of his weaker brothers. Certainly this tendency has made the Church a target for much natural and understandable bitterness from those outside the fold who might have been won to her by a little collective humility. It is puzzling to these people how pride can be recognized and called sinful in a person, but made a virtue when referred to an institution; how humility is so necessary in the individual but unnecessary in the Mystical Body; how Christ had it but His Church has not.

Since there has been a misunderstanding of Christian love, which had to be purely spiritual or considered evil, there is a tendency now to err in the opposite direction. There seems to be so much clamor against celibacy. It is called a deterrent to true human love. This is the purest rot! If Christ recommended it, as He undoubtedly did, it was not because it was a deterrent to the very thing He said was to contain the whole law and the prophets. If it has become so, then something is radically wrong. And it has become so. But as the inexperienced doctor is apt to grasp at the obvious symptoms and misdiagnose the sickness, so the honest critic of the absence of love in the very Church which was founded on love is apt to blame the celibacy of the clergy and the cold praise of the loveless virgin in the catalog of saints. One should realize that if celibacy and chastity do not increase the capacity for true love, then they have failed as virtues. But virtues do not fail; people fail, especially people without virtue. The withdrawn celibate, however technically chaste he may be, does lack the warmth of charity, of virtue, unless of course, like most withdrawn people, he is just sick.

Many objecting to celibacy insist that a man needs a woman to share his thoughts, words, and deeds, his aspirations, to bring out the best in him. It should be obvious that a man who does not need a woman is not a candidate for celibacy; he is a natural bachelor. But having a woman does not guarantee personal fulfillment. Many a married man still needs a woman to share his aspirations. No man is so lonely as the man who is lonely in bed with his own wife, and he is by no means a rarity. Many insist that celibacy often drives a priest to alcoholism, and the oblivion of escape. But marriage also drives many to alcoholism, and celibacy is often called an escape from matrimony. Alcoholism drives many men to the state of celibacy if not to the virtue of chastity. Alcoholics are not noted as good husbands, or wives either, but it is not their state which leads them to alcoholism but their personal inadequacy. Their problem is escape from responsibility, not the acceptance of it which is involved in both celibacy and the married state. It is not easy to pinpoint specific causes for these problems, but it is human to grab the first likely looking culprit. It is easy to blame celibacy for the problems of the celibate, but too many people in that state have developed to a real stature as human beings for celibacy to be blamed. Let us face it; it is just about as hard to be faithful to one woman as it is to have none. There are too many men in the world to whom position, money, liquor, drugs, or even their own ease mean much more than women, for celibacy to be made the villain of unhappiness in the priesthood. Failure to keep a promise or a vow does not mean that it was a mistake to make the promise or the vow in the first place. It only shows that human weakness is human weakness, and the path to success is littered with failure. While for many, pride may make chastity an easier thing than contrition for sins of the flesh, still the happiest priests are those who through celibacy learned to love deeply and well.

Few priests who are unhappily celibate now will find themselves more happily married, when the novelty has worn off. The impassioned plea of a man now a priest for the one thing through which he thinks he will become a whole man, marriage, is a sorry joke. This man has never been a whole man in the priesthood and will hardly be so in the married state, but he will have one thing less to blame for his already emotionally crippled life. No one thing can mature a man; nor can any one thing keep a man from maturing. No man can find his fulfillment in any one thing, any more than he can have a healthy, well-built body living on one kind of food, or be well educated by studying only one subject. Furthermore, his approach to marriage will more than likely be the same approach he made to his life in the priesthood, not a very satisfactory one. There are enough marriages in the world to show that marriage in itself does not mature a man. It can help, but in the same way that facing up to his responsibilities helps a man to mature in the priesthood. Willingness to face responsibilities is the best sign of maturability. The congenitally irresponsible are immaturable, celibate or married. The problem of celibacy in the priesthood is not the problem of undertaking a career in which one cannot mature, but of being mature enough to undertake a career demanding the giving and receiving of great love, using all the drive, interest, and zest that God-given sex provides even when not fully exercised as in marriage.

Unfortunately, because a man is by nature sexual, and because all human love has the sexual factor involved, many unwittingly assume that to be sexual is to be human, and to be human is to be sexual; therefore sexuality must dominate in human love. Thus, in the interest of maintaining a technical chastity, many through ignorance have made love an occasion of sin, a danger to, and a contradiction of, chastity. In doing so they have at once robbed love of its greatest quality, chastity, and have made it impossible for the celibate to enter into a meaningful adult relationship. They would have him remain a child. Apart from that, Christ's unequivocal command was to love, and the advice of these misguided guides is to love not, without any apparent sense of conflict with Christ's teaching. Again, any realist knows that there is an incredible amount of sex without love, and much wonderful human love without sex dominating the relationship. Prudes are shocked when, from time to time, cases of incest make the news. They get vicarious satisfaction from the lurid details which they would not miss reading. They would deny the reality of a basic sexuality in the parental-filial or fraternal relationship. They do not see that the sexual polarity has to be there even though normally in modern society it is controlled. Many would deny that the honest normal sexual inclinations of the celibate can likewise be controlled, given sufficient love.

It is a fact that the marriage that is primarily sex-oriented and secondarily love-oriented is on shaky ground. Marriage depends far more on love than on sex for its continuation. One can hardly doubt this when he sees the vaunted "sex bombs" of the movie industry leap-frogging from marriage to marriage, each of which was to be "the marriage of my life." Some of these marriages do endure for weeks or months, and at times even for a few years. Few of them last long enough to merit even the metaphorical adjective "eternal." Living with these people even for a short time might well seem an eternity to some.

Celibacy is a very maturing thing, and of course it is a vocation for the mature man. If a man is to do without the full use of sex all his life, he must be mature because it is one of the basics of human living. To live without it the celibate, like the blind man who compensates in his other senses for the loss of one, has to compensate in his life for the absence of something so fundamental. He has to be more of a man, not less, to do this adequately. When he does so, he is very happy and very productive indeed. When he does not he is very unhappy. And that unhappiness comes from the very qualities in his life which make celibacy impossible, the inability to place his real needs before his whims, the failure of his purposes to surmount his desires.

The only real argument for "a married clergy" in the western Church, as opposed to some clergy who are married, is that, through circumstances made plain by an obvious clerical shortage, celibacy should be abandoned. However, to repeat, the present "obvious" shortage does not come from the shortage of priests but rather from the wasteful employment of priests in so many fields not requiring holy orders. Add to this the number of priests not working fully at priestly work, and the shortage is much more apparent than real. There is also no reason why exceptions should not be made for men of high caliber who, though married, would be considered desirable in the priesthood. Some of these exceptions would work out and others would not, but the average of the celibate clergy would be maintained.

There are those who naïvely distinguish between religious who would continue with celibacy and the secular or diocesan priests who would marry. There are as many failures among religious priests in this matter as there are among diocesan priests, perhaps because they are less worldly-wise, or because they too lack the evidence that happy marriages are made by happy, not unhappy, people.

Among the more vocal proponents of a married clergy are those who claim that not many priests adjust well to celibacy. If they mean to say that not many enjoy or revel in their celibacy, they are correct. There has to be something wrong with a man who enjoys a sexless life. No one expects an army officer to enjoy leaving his wife and family to fight in Vietnam, where undoubtedly some good officers are faithful to their wives. A priest is not supposed to enjoy celibacy, but merely to vow it for life for the love of God and the many one can serve better for being celibate. It's a fact that one is freer to love others when he is not married, and this does not call for the snide remark but for respect. The price of loving others truly, of having the capacity to see and fulfill the true needs of others, is a high one which assures real love and not some cheap facsimile. It surely was not the intention of Christ when He proffered the invitation to celibacy that it be an easy and a comfortable way of life. But it was to be a good way with the happiness that a truly good way can provide.

If someone could prove that in the ranks of the married clergy there is less infidelity than among celibates there might be a point. The point would not be that celibacy should be done away with, but that celibates should be better prepared for their lives by effective instruction and understanding, that the selection of men for the celibate priesthood should be more discriminating and less frantic, that mere children should not be taken from their homes to seminaries, and that academic qualification is not the only way to judge a man fit for the priesthood.

Those who think celibates less able to counsel married people would think one could not understand atomic energy because he could not personally build the bomb. It is a fact that most married men do not understand their wives, so it is even more difficult for them to counsel others' wives. The counselor should be mature. How many men in any walk of life, married or single, are mature? How many are capable of the fairly objective appraisal of themselves, let alone others, that is demanded of counselors? The married counselor can learn from his own marriage, but he also can be so badly misled by his unfortunate marriage that he could not in honesty recommend that way of life. There are those who quite honestly believe that marriage does little but take the joy out of sex. That they are wrong does not change the fact that they have let their own experiences and capacities mislead them. A man is not better qualified to counsel others because he is not a celibate, but there is an outside chance that the celibate can be a more impersonal and objective referee.

From the signs of the times, there might well be a married clergy in the western Church within fifteen years. If so, it will be a tragedy not unmixed with blessings. There will be many good and wonderful married clergy dedicated to God and His work in the Church, but, nature being nature, terrible conflicts will arise and undo much of that work. The emphasis will be on continuation rather than growth, development, and the raising of men to the highest level. The prestige of Christianity will sink to a depth not reached in years. The loss to the Church might never be recouped. Leadership through the years of the "sexual revolution" will be in default, when an emotionally sick world needs to see the beauty of chastity which contains the discipline required to raise sex to the stature of love. This leadership can only come from mature human beings capable of and willing to undertake the celibate life with its challenges and its happiness.

At any rate, open-minded dialogue must continue on this subject. Nothing that could be good for the Church or souls should be excluded from the dialogue. Every realistic adjustment to the promotion of Christ's teachings and way of life should be unhesitatingly made. But all is wasted if the way of life of His representatives and leaders is not inspiring publicly and privately. For it is a fact that the world never needed Christ more than it needs Him now. And He should be as well represented as possible. Yes, by men willing to give up all things for Him, not only women, but position, worldly distinction, money, and sometimes perhaps even smoking or golf where these things represent the self-indulgence which conflicts with the fuller dedication to Jesus Christ.

The greatest obstacle to chastity in the priesthood of America is unquestionably prosperity, money in the pocket of the priest. When Christ recommended chastity He surely did not intend that we take it so seriously as to forget that He also recommended poverty. The priest who makes the legal, technical, but utterly incongruous distinction between the priest with the vow of poverty and the priest without the vow of poverty is only begging the question. Nothing in the Christian religion can dispense any priest from practicing the virtue of poverty. When it is said that no priest who ever practiced poverty had trouble with chastity it is quickly pointed out that priests living in poverty are as quick to fall as those living in luxury, if not quicker. But there is a great difference between living in poverty and practicing the virtue of poverty. The priest who has no choice in the matter cannot be said to be practicing virtue when he lives in poverty. It is when a man can have nearly anything he wants in the world that the idea of doing without a woman becomes increasingly difficult. And in the opulence of America, the priest can, through the generosity of the people and sources available to him, have most of the ordinary luxuries of life, even some of the extraordinary ones. A house may belong to the diocese, but the priest or the bishop lives in it. It is not owned personally by its occupant, but many a rectory is a very luxurious home. The priest who has not the discernment to practice the virtue of poverty in his life, will also not have the discernment to see when he is passing even good taste in the appointments of his house or his living. The fact, often wryly pointed out, that the married clergy of other denominations have their better halves does not justify the better quarters of the celibates, though some of them may be a compensation of sorts.

Poverty has not been made a great virtue in the priesthood, but it was the condition of the vocation of the rich young man of the Gospel. Even when missionaries are living in poverty (along with virtually whole nations and whole peoples), as are many priests in the same diocese with those who live luxuriously, the luxury-lovers have little sense of shame, wrongdoing, or even lack of virtue. Few of them are kept awake at night by the specter of the world's starving millions. The fact remains, which no priest could possibly escape, that if Jesus Christ is not the model for the priest then no one is, and nothing in religion or out of it matters very much except the comfort of the priest. Christ was poor and lived poorly. It is as simple as that.

Much to the credit of those who see and admit this fact of poverty in theory and in practice, the personal money of the priest is being carefully considered. The whole question of Mass intentions, stole fees, and the personal income of the priests is being rethought. The underlying problem is not one of Mass intentions or the other perquisites of office, but rather one of virtue. No one wants to see the priests out on the streets with their begging bowls, but the law is no replacement for the virtue which the law is powerless to legislate. And until virtue, not the black suit and white collar, is the identification mark of the priest, no legislation can possibly make Christianity an effective force. Just as worship in the vernacular cannot accomplish the change required of a true Christian's heart, neither can the councils or decrees make the changes required in the hearts of the priests of Jesus Christ. Nor can any priest afford to wait until the other priests reform; virtue is much too important for that, and the failure to improve is much too consequential a matter for delay.

What, then, is the priest in reality? One can say that he is a man appointed to offer sacrifice to God on behalf of the people. But this describes the role of the priest; it does not say what he is. The priest is, first and foremost, a man of charity. Not a man who gives the crumbs from his table but a man who has pledged to give himself. And if he does not, then St. Paul can describe him with a single word — he is "nothing." It is very hard to be less than that! Charity is love, the gift of oneself to God and to others. Where charity has fled the lives of the priests it is generally because they allowed themselves to be told what the demands of real charity in their lives meant. No man can tell another man what charity demands of him. It is something he must see and understand for himself, and then make his choice to give or to withhold.

The priest is a mere human being aspiring to a state of life demanding unusual dedication, made reasonable only in the light of divine revelation or faith in God, entailing great personal sacrifice in this world and an infinitely satisfying reward in eternity. Sacrifice without its rewards is insane. The idea of sacrifice meaning happiness is appalling to selfish people, but that is because, as people, they are appalling. Christ's promise of happiness in this world is too often overlooked in the unfortunate tendency of Christians to downgrade this experienced world when comparing it to an unexperienced heaven. However, Christ was very clear in His promise of happiness in this world for the man who could put aside his personal wishes, likes, and ambitions for the establishment of the kingdom of God in the hearts of men. The fulfillment of that promise has been expressed well by the adage that "virtue is its own reward." Men of real virtue have far more peace and happiness in this world than any other people. Those who would deny this have never really tried virtue.

The unhappy priest is certainly not a man of virtue in the true sense of the word. He has no power over himself and so has to be the victim of his emotions. He is not a realist, is not truthful. He is a dreamer, torn apart by his efforts to find meaning in his dreams. Ultimately he has to face the fact that there is no one to blame for his state but himself. The priest making an honest effort to live the life knows happiness. He has in his life love unequalled in the lives of most others primarily because he has been capable of the sacrifice occasioned by love.

Happiness in the life of the priest comes from love, as it does in the life of anyone else. The good priest has many times the love and satisfaction even of parents who, in the return of love from their children, find a joy which their love for each other can never bring. Again, the world is in obvious and headlong flight from loneliness. Yet the innumerable lonely people would be happy if only someone needed them, wanted them. But since most lonely people are selfish, who needs them? The world passes them by because they live off it greedily, contributing so very little to it besides their presence. The priest who is unwanted by his people is indeed a monument of selfishness. The priest giving himself to his people seldom feels any loneliness except that of the man who cannot be filled with material pleasure. People need him more than the doctor who cares for their physical well-being. The priest who is not loved can attribute it to a single cause. He is living for himself in a calling that demands that he live for others. He covets the esteem of Christ without the likeness to Christ. He thinks there is some magic way of being like Christ without living as Christ lived. It would be easier for him to walk on water. Yet, strange as it may seem, this realization has escaped countless priests in the course of the very training calculated to make them Christlike.

The faults and failings of priests are the faults and failings of human beings. There must have been some reason why Christ chose human beings to direct His Church. It surely was not to glorify human weakness. It must have been because only human beings could show their fellowmen how high they could rise despite every human weakness. And the glory of the Church does lie in its humanity as well as its divinity. The Church in the world is a continuing hypostatic union, Christ living in the world in His people. Many people are content to worship God from afar, to see His awful majesty from as great a distance as possible, to let His influence in their lives be the necessary minimum. But that was not the way that God would have it. He sent His Son, not merely to be with us, but to be one of us, one with us. And when that Son was made man, He said that He was not only one of us, but that He was our fellowman. God is to be worshiped in our next-door neighbor, who is to be given every courtesy that Christ would be given. It is on this very point that man has failed, that Christianity has foundered. Man is still telling God how far he will go in charity, when God has told him he must go all the way.

The power of God within the human Church is no more hidden today than was the divinity of Christ to those around Him. The power of the Church to raise men to a life above dead selfishness is just as evident as was the power of Christ on earth to raise the dead to life. His message at that time in raising the dead was that He could raise the spiritually dead if they were interested. But the people did not take kindly to the message. Those who want to justify themselves today by the human failings of the Church do not take too kindly to the truth it teaches. They are like the people who found Christ's learning and power baffling because He was only the son of Mary and Joseph the carpenter. It is hard for any man to see the things he does not want to see. The priest is no exception. He too needs the touch of Christ on his eyes if they are to be opened. And they will be if he asks. He too must really want to see. Sooner or later the priests of America, like the priests of the world, will have to cry out humbly to God, "Lord, that I may see." If they do, they will quickly learn that they can do all things in Him who strengthens them.

Anyone who wants to know what is wrong with the Church today should not underestimate the number of priests who think Christ's promises of fulfillment are actually empty ones. They sooner or later choose between those promises and the world's pleasure. How then can they possibly be happy?

Chapter 3

Vocations and the Seminaries

WHEN St. Charles Borromeo saw the chaotic state of the priesthood and resolved that seminaries should be established for the better preparation and education of priests, he rendered a service to the Church which can hardly be overestimated. The benefits of his work are being reaped to the present day. It is a great tribute to St. Charles, if not to modern authorities, that only now, after three hundred years, is the necessity of updating his work being faced.

No man likes to see in himself the source of his troubles. Parents who have problems with their children are always eager to attribute these troubles to the schools the children attend. However, every child is born of his first teacher and into his first classroom. The parents are the teachers and the home is the school. Seldom can anything counteract the influence of those teachers and that school. Nor can parents reasonably expect the schools to do the work they either cannot or will not do themselves. Regardless of the defects in seminaries, and they are many, it must be admitted that no seminary ever took a good boy who wanted very much to be a good priest and ruined him. But it is the work of the seminary to take the average boy and to try to inspire him with the desire to be more than an average priest, contributing everything possible to that end. The failure to do this is what is making a reexamination of the seminaries, their staffs and their policies, essential. But before examining the seminaries, the matter and the theology of vocation itself have to be faced.

In recent times few churches in the world have not echoed some formal and official prayer for vocations to the priesthood and the religious life. There seems to be an urgency bordering on panic about providing more priests. Yet experience has already shown that were the supply of candidates a small percentage larger and of slightly better quality many bishops would arbitrarily, perhaps capriciously, decide there were enough. They would decline whatever candidates were available without reference to the Holy Spirit. Few of them, indeed, would feel constrained to supply the world beyond the borders of their dioceses with good priests, or to qualify enough good priests within their dioceses for the intensive cultivation of deep spirituality and effective religion there. Many priests who are aware of this, in the face of orders from the highest Church authorities to storm heaven for vocations, shake their heads in something between disbelief and disgust. Why should God be called upon to eliminate the consequences of human negligence? Should God be forced by prayer to bless human dullness, disinterest, and stupidity, so that small men can glory in themselves and forget their need of Him? Are there no penalties to be paid for error and blindness? Is God to be bribed by self-interested prayer to take irresponsible men off the hook? Even if the shortage is what God wills, and there is just as much chance that it is as that it is not, is not the problem more fundamental than that? It is a case again of praying to God for rain when He would have man use his brains, energy, and much of the money he wastes on war and luxury to bring water from the ground, or to irrigate the deserts of the world. If man's prayers to God were answered at the whim of man, God's relationship to man would be reversed.

The problem of vocations must be tackled from a much more realistic point of view than that of panic-stricken letters from the chanceries demanding public prayers for something which is almost exclusively the result of private prayer. Vocation is the result of the union of the mind and heart with God, of prayer. It is the result of grace in the God-loving soul. This grace of love alone can make a young man or woman undertake for life to put God and His work in the foremost place of importance. Vocation is simply the normal result of the love of God in the heart of a man. When that love reaches a certain intensity there is nothing else to do but leave all else behind and cleave to God, much the same way as a young man, for the love of a special woman, leaves mother and father and cleaves to his wife.

To the rich young man, now made famous by the Gospel story of his rejection of vocation, Christ replied: "If you will be perfect, go and sell what you have and give to the poor, and come follow me." While much has been rightly made of this illustration used by Christ, the point of it is usually missed. Typically, the reader is impressed by all that was asked of the young man, rather than by all that was offered to him. For his paltry riches he was offered priceless perfection, God, the author of all riches. It was a bargain by objective standards, too expensive only by subjective ones.

Herein lies the first stumbling block to quality and quantity of vocations. Those who urge young people to give up everything for Christ seem peculiarly blind to something which is much too obvious to the young people. The vocation-seekers quite wrongly assume that, since they themselves have become priests, they have left all to follow Christ. In many cases they have, with the ingenuity of inherently selfish men, managed to obtain most of the good things of both worlds. Certainly, if celibacy is abandoned the last vestiges of giving up anything will have disappeared.

This is nowhere better illustrated than in the man reveling in the role of monsignor, whose image is by far the worst in the Church. The Council Fathers tried desperately to point out the contradiction of the dedicated Christian seeking or even being "rewarded" by empty titles and millinery (as the late Cardinal Mooney used to call it), but they did not succeed. When one considers the number of parish priests who are, or would like to be, monsignors, it is understandable that young people do not find them inspiring vocation-wise. Certainly, not all monsignors fit this category. There have been many good men of integrity who had no desire for this "signal" honor. However, when they expressed the desire to the bishop to forgo it, they were commanded under obedience to be present at the "investiture," which itself must be extemporaneously composed because, thank God, there is no explicit form for such a fiasco in the Ritual. The "order" to accept an "honor" violates the most basic concept of freedom, and it would not be tolerated were it not backed up by the implicit threat of discrimination if ignored.

This issue may be dismissed as a minor point, but it is not so minor if many of the Fathers of the Council earnestly wanted something done about it. It is not so minor that it is lost on many of the young people. It is not so minor when it can be even jokingly said that when one man gets the purple eight men get the blues. One young man, when he realized that he had been had by being made a monsignor, burst out and said, "Why don't they do away with these traps?" It was suggested to him that it were better that young priests be clear-sighted enough to avoid them.

All these things militate against the real happiness of priests. There will be no dearth of vocations when the priests are obviously happy and fulfilled men. Nor will there be any shortage the day that priests are really the servants of the people. The appetite of young people for service is astounding in this day and age of the surfeit of good things. The Peace Corps, Poverty Corps, Job Corps, and many other organizations dedicated to the help and welfare of others have many volunteers. It has become obvious that when many of the corporal works of mercy of the Church became money-makers, such as hospitals, private schools, and rest homes, leadership began to pass into the hands of the laity. The good Samaritan, after all, was a layman.

Little or nothing can be done about these situations as long as the charity of priests and religious is bonded to the bishops and the superiors of orders whose policies are dictated by business principles, brick and mortar expansion, and material development. Perhaps the era of the new and Christian religious life will come when religious are personally given their salaries for working in institutes under civil authorities. Then they can come home and pay their board in the religious houses in which they reside, live poorly (modestly, not in abject poverty), pay their taxes as everyone else does, buy their own necessities and use the rest of it for works of charity, as they see best.

The word vocation itself indicates the belief that a priest or religious receives a special "call" from God to give his life to "His service." This call was considered to be something between a gentle motion toward the priesthood and an almost unavoidable compulsion to it. Grace was generally considered to be a sort of other-world divine fuel, operating mysteriously, like atomic energy to the layman, God's finger triggering it. Certainly it was not commonly considered as coming through the ordinary circumstances of time, place, and the people around. Now, in a more realistic and enlightened age, theologically as well as scientifically, vocation is considered more and more to be simply an extension of the calling of the Christian, by baptism, to be a child of God. Every human being must love God, is called to love God. Baptism makes one a child of

God. Therefore, through baptism the child is bound by love to God just as truly as human birth establishes a child-parent relationship of love and responsibility. The vocation to the priesthood is the development of that love to the degree that the child is led to dedicate himself for life primarily to God and His work. There can be no doubt that this love is especially nurtured in good homes with responsible and loving parents and in good schools with dedicated teachers who educate the whole boy in all aspects of his life, including religion. These are some of the circumstantial graces of vocation. But it has been considered ideal to take a child when he is young and bring all these good influences to bear on him in the hope that a vocation will be the normal outgrowth. Now we are beginning to see that to do so is to take unfair advantage of the child and to evoke decision from him at an age in which he is neither capable of making a lasting decision nor mature enough to understand sufficiently what is involved in it.

With puberty there is the beginning of the loving process which extends itself from pets, boys, girls, men, and women right up to God Himself. Nor does the child appreciate the difference in these loves. Thus the state of fervor in the child is apt to be overrated. Just as the usual revivalist conversion of Protestant children closely follows puberty and the outburst of emotional love, so the first real "signs" of vocation are seen in the Catholic teens. Every priest knows the response he gets when he goes into a class of grade school children and asks how many of them intend to be priests or nuns. The positive and overwhelming response becomes more and more negative and doubtful as the years go on and the children pass into adolescence and adulthood. Other forces are beginning to compete. Many feel that unless the work of religion is done before the competition sets in, there will be fewer and fewer vocations. This is unfair to the child and, of course, unfair to religion. It grossly underestimates the power of grace, the ability of divine providence to take care of it.

One of the direct results of this beat-the-competition theory is the confusion of vocation with escape. The problem of disastrous teen-age marriages has made it plain that many children from unhappy and emotionally disturbing homes have used marriage as a means of escape from the home. Their unhappiness has militated against the children's proper education, leading often to such a degree of emotional disturbance that they are uneducable. These children are desperate to get away from their homes. Since they have neither the age nor the other qualifications necessary to get a job which would make them independent, they look to love and marriage as the route of escape. The love that is denied them at home they think they can find in the arms of other immature children in the same love-starved condition as themselves. Having only the physical qualifications for motherhood and fatherhood, they undertake roles for which they are unfitted in almost every other way. By their very early twenties they have three or four children. They suddenly realize that they have had none of the fun of growing up. Embittered, they see life passing them by, and decide that it must not be. The marriage actually or virtually ends there and their children are abandoned, thrown loveless into a world where they need love more than anything else. And so another generation of emotional cripples is born. This route of escape from the unhappy home is so obvious in the modern sociological setup that it cannot be denied. However, what is not so evident is that the vocation to religious life can also be used as an avenue of escape from home.

There are young boys and girls with a deep sense of religious devotion who come from unhappy homes, or homes in which, for some reason, they are not given the love they need and want. They have found love in religion just as truly as many of the others have found it in physical love. Therefore they want to be priests or nuns. They have been daily communicants, and so, with the blessings of their parish priests, they leave at an early age for the seminaries or convents. In these places there is enough education, living comfort, interest, and hope of happiness, along with the normal religious rewards of good living, to keep them going. However, when they reach real maturity they often begin to wonder whether they have chosen well. Even if they have vocations they are frequently unprepared for this normal doubt, and the new surge of desire for the world and the things it presents for their enjoyment. They begin to feel resentment at having been deliberately isolated from these hidden joys. They are almost ready to believe that these pleasures were deliberately misrepresented to them so that they would ignore them and look only to religious life. From underrating these pleasures they begin to overestimate them, often approaching them naïvely and unrealistically. Unhappiness can become their lot. In this state, religious disillusionment does nothing for them in the lean years of their religious lives. They lose sight of the fact that such lean years are as normal as the difficult years of marriage, which if lived through courageously and with principle make the later years of marriage a source of great peace and joy to the persevering husband and wife. People who have lived by their emotions are incapable of enduring the lean years, let alone profiting by them.

The idea of vocation has to be rethought in the light of a world from which religious persons can no longer remain isolated. They are not to leave the world but to go to it as Christ did. If the Church is essentially apostolic, its best people must be so. Then the incredible phenomenon of a religious, who knows nothing about the world, telling people how to live in it or, even worse, telling them how little it has to offer, will be a thing of the past. The sweet young nun explaining the facts of life about which she knows nothing to keen young teen-agers will be an impossibility. Religious people who know what they are talking about and who have come to grips with reality will be the effective force. And we must have professional religious who know what they are talking about. Generally we are not going to get them by searching out the immature, naïve, and unspoiled, and training them in a way which our critics with some justification call brainwashing. We are not going to get them from the ranks of the emotional cripples who fill the world, many of whom have helped to fill the ranks of the clergy and the nuns. Brainwashing is still brainwashing even though not intended. Pessimists feel that mature and effective priests will not be found if youth is not exploited. They fear that college and its fruits, education and the promise of affluence, are too heady an influence to permit vocations to thrive. They fear that religion is on the wane, or cannot command a real place in a practical world. This is a strange fear in a confused world so obviously in need of religion and God. That need is so clear that it is hard to credit anyone with much objectivity who doubts it.

The grave concern about the shortage of vocations is only partly understandable in the face of the uneconomic use of priests and religious. Until present times when the shortage has been acutely felt, religious were generally equated with cheap labor. Very able administrators, for the sake of cost and perhaps humility, were tied to chores anyone could have done. And talents which could have been better used in the work of the Church were left undeveloped because of cost or the danger of pride. This led to a great deal of unnecessary personal frustration and disrespect for the rule. Cheap labor, as the economic facts of life easily show, often is expensive. Cheap labor which is contented is most often lazy, ineffective, or unproductive. As one priest put it, "If we had enough priests, what would those do who are now doing nothing?" To which another replied, "They would each have an assistant." Having diocesan priests teaching algebra and geometry in high schools for no other reason than dollars and cents is a tragic and short-sighted policy. Having priests tied up even in seminaries where lay people would serve equally well or better is wasteful. The great need of American Catholics is to have their priests available for the things that really matter. Running parish clubs, supervising buildings, organizing financial drives, or administering charity organizations are not important enough to keep the priests unavailable to their people. The unhappy aspect of the priest-worker movement is that it involves reaching people who would not have been lost to the Church had priests in the first place done the work for which they were ordained. If the priests were available to the people for the things the people need most from them — guidance, direction, maintenance of the spiritual flavor of their lives — means could be found for the jobs which are now taking the priests away from their real work. The priest as an executive has too often replaced the priest as a spiritual father. This has been largely the fault of the seminaries which, regardless of what is said in justification of their work, have not qualified the spiritual fathers for spiritual fatherhood and its responsibilities.

There is no greater challenge to the Church than the challenge facing the seminaries. What to do with the candidates for the priesthood? How should they be handled? How should they be trained? This challenge calls for the wisdom of a Solomon, the spirituality of an angel, the vision of an eagle, the courage of a lion, and the strength of an ox. Therefore it is a challenge which must not be left with the priority rating of an elective operation. If the bishops of America think an annual statement is worth the trouble of meeting once a year, they should certainly consider that their seminaries merit a meeting once a year if they are to operate on something better than Roman directives, episcopal whims, and the moment-to-moment decisions of a harried rector. Nor is it sufficient to let authority pass into the hands of the proletariat by default. The seminary which lacks the inspiration of leadership can serve neither youth nor the Church well. From it can come only an uninspired and uninspiring priesthood.

Modern seminary training has never come up with either a spirituality for the diocesan priest or a spirituality for the laity. It has been traditionally left to the canonical "religious" to be spiritual people. The child who seems to be "spiritual" is marked by bystanders for a "religious" vocation. Insofar as they have had any spiritual training, the diocesan priests have been trained in monastic spirituality. And insofar as this is real spirituality, it is not very suitable for the secular clergy nor to the life its members lead. It is freely admitted that this is so by most priests who care. Generally those priests who have been fortunate enough to remain "spiritual" have too often done so at the cost of their effectiveness as involved priests, close to their people, deeply interested in and available to them. This is substantiated by the consistency with which the laity refer to the cold, withdrawn, ascetical type of priest as a holy man. The uncontaminated, separated man rather than the warm, interested priest impresses the laity with his holiness, if not his charity, which they do not identify as holiness.

The significance of prayer will best differentiate the spirituality of the old order from that of the new. Prayer, to the monastically trained priest, is that time set aside for God from a busy day. And let there be no mistake, this sacrosanct prayer-life has been the recognized sign of priestliness regardless of its cost to the apostolate or its natural attraction for the spiritual "loner." Yet prayer for the diocesan priest must be the gift of himself to God and his fellowman in the selflessness of true charity. What else can the exhortation to pray without ceasing mean, or to pray always? That religious life will have its period of formal prayer goes without saying; that it will be a monastic routine is impossible. The virtual impossibility of regularity in his formal prayer-life has been used by the diocesan priest as a dispensation from charity, the gift of himself to his people. He cannot or will not take time from his recreation for his people. And as long as it is basic recreation in the sense of needed rest or change, he should not. But then his chores take the rest of his time, and his people get the crumbs. Since he cannot give even God the time he has learned should be given, the people don't matter too much.

Unless the secular clergy bases its spirituality on real charity, however it may be defined, real spirituality will be an anomaly in the priesthood. Few priests question that the monastic formation is wasted on the average candidate for holy orders, who will spend his life in the active ministry. The most consequential factor in the monastic type of spiritual formation of priests is the inability of those priests to develop their spirituality in the field of charity. This has led to a worldly rather than a spiritual laity, a pious laity whose religion is churchiness, not charity, personal, not public, self-oriented, not neighbor-oriented.

The monastic spiritual formation makes too much of self-scrutiny and too little of integrity, honesty, responsibility, and generosity. One of the fundamentals of monastic spirituality is guidance and direction by competent people in the ways of spiritual growth. The guide has tended to outrank the Holy Spirit. While the desirability of guidance cannot be questioned, utter dependence on it can and should be. And in seminaries, from the beginning, there is all too little competence in this field. Yet when the young priest leaves the seminary he hopes for the availability of directors among his fellow priests. He spends time looking and finding almost none. Facing the reality of lack of spirituality, he then easily dispenses himself from spirituality. He excuses himself from the obligation to progress in virtue because he tried to find a suitable director and could not. They are simply not available. He has not been trained to be available to the very real motions of the Holy Spirit. (Although it is not the point here, the lack of spiritual directors for the nuns is even more disastrous. The trained overdependence on them, coupled with their lack and/or unavailability, is what has allowed the tyrannical intrusion of customs and routines on the nuns' personal freedom, to say nothing of their dreadfully detailed supervision by superiors. The Holy Spirit has gone generally unrecognized in their lives too. There has not only been a dearth of directors for them, but there has been even a lack of efficacious interest in providing them.) Students can go through a seminary without a single spiritual word said to them by their spiritual director. The basic cause of this is the choice of seminary staff from newly ordained priests sent on for their doctorates. Academically inclined, and just returned from doctoral work to the seminary, they have nothing spiritual to say. They could not prepare men for spiritual priestly lives because they do not know and seldom get to really know what priestly life is.

Contributing to this situation in the seminaries is the fact that ascetical theology has not been taken very seriously. Yet seminarians are taught that it is the science of the saints, that it is the theology of the spiritual life, that their holiness of life will depend on it to a large degree. Frequently the most inadequate professor on the staff is the professor of ascetical theology. The time given to it is minimal, out of all proportion to its importance in the life of the priest and those he will direct.

A comparable situation exists in Catholic high schools where a serious study is being made of the effect of religious education on the students. Since there is a tremendous demand for higher academic standards which directors are anxious to provide, the best brains, talent, and general competence are put into the academic subjects on which the school accreditation depends. These are mathematics, science, literature, languages, etc. Who teaches religion? Often it is a venerable, superannuated member of a religious community who is qualified to teach nothing else. If one has been a religious for a number of years it is "presumed" that one knows religion. It is also "presumed" that one can teach it. The results have been a disaster when one considers that the children are in Catholic schools primarily to get a good grounding in the principles of their religion.

If the latest studies of the matter correctly indicate that only a "moderate but statistically significant" relationship exists between Catholic education and adult religious behavior, and that "Catholic education is virtually wasted on three fourths of those in Catholic schools because of the absence of a sufficiently religious family milieu," it must be because religion did not matter that much to them, and few who taught it could make it matter.

There are many subjects in seminary training which matter less than ascetical theology or the spiritual life but which are given adequate time and thought. Nothing should take priority over this subject because spirituality is the one thing which the world wants from the clergy, which the people of God have a right to expect from their priests. Men need a reason for fighting their real but misleading desires; a man has to have cause to do violence to himself. Sense has to be made of so many apparently senseless situations and circumstances which are spiritually meaningful but materially unacceptable. The searching mind of a spiritual man can do this. Evidence of spiritual undernourishment in the seminary lies in the fact that so many young priests come to their work as if the search were over, not just beginning. In discussion of the question with some three hundred priests over a ten-year period, over ninety percent of them indicated that they read one or less spiritual books a year.

One of the most serious problems of seminaries is their very rigid control from Rome. The Curia has reserved to itself the decisions about almost every detail of seminary formation. This has led to inflexibility, an air of untouchableness about its staff, which at once holds them sacred and gives the impression of their superiority without question or examination. Yet few of the men exercising this control have seen the world outside of Italy, let alone familiarized themselves with the requirements of the ministry in that world outside. The Italian system has prevailed in the formation of priests destined to live and work in conditions diametrically opposed to those of Italy. Certainly if there is any group of men who ought to know what they want in their priests it should be the collective bishops of the nation or culture in which the priests are working. Then, too, monopoly minimizes progress. There must be two, three, or five ways to prepare priests for their work. There should be enough variation and scope allowed in training to learn through trial and error, to make practical tests which would clearly show the advantages and flaws in ways and means. There should be room for competition to show what succeeds and what fails. On the contrary, there has been not only detailed control from Rome, but also intransigence toward any suggestions from outside seminaries, even through normal channels, and this, regardless of how basically sensible or praiseworthy the suggestions.

This system is also reflected in the dioceses. A seminary appointment is generally an episcopal appointment. Most bishops want to retain complete control of their seminaries. This is not healthy. It stifles their growth and development. It limits drastically the qualifications of the staff. It assures a low standard of education for the specific area served by the seminary. Seminaries should not be diocesan but regional; they should be controlled not by a single bishop but by a board of bishops, with a number of highly qualified priests and laity, including religious women as well as laywomen, with decisive votes. This would not take the ruling authority from the bishops but it would assure the hearing of the priests, religious, and laity in this matter of greatest importance. The staff should consist of people from every diocese served by the seminary, assuring the best men from a diocese for seminary work, or at least men well qualified for the work they do. There should be an eagerness among the staff to compete in excellence, an eagerness to do a good job, rather than a reconciliation to the drudgery and oblivion often part of seminary work.

The seminary staff should have competent articulate lay people, male and female, sharing equal status with the clerical staff. The tardiness of the Church in acknowledging that at least half its members are women, and that the largest number, by far, of its professionally dedicated people are women, does nothing to support its boast that it is responsible for the elevated status of women in the world. It is not that a concerted effort toward clerical coeducation should be encouraged. It is just that women have been completely ostracized from the administration of the Church regardless of their talents and undoubted qualifications, excepting of course the kitchen and domestic services of seminaries and episcopal palaces. It remains almost beyond credibility that all the legislation governing women in the Church has been made by men virtually without consultation with women. That until recently this could be said of all international and national civil law does not change the fact that the situation still persists in the Church. No seminary staff should be without some women professors. Not only might they bring a little refinement where it is sadly needed, but among the desirable by-products would be the stimulus of intelligent, competent women working with a staff long protected from the competition which might embarrass it into better work. It was the mentality which considered women inferior that let the calendar reach the year 1911 before the first female religious was admitted to a Catholic institution of learning at the college level. Were it not for the pressure of the outside world, she might not have arrived there yet.

Catholic seminaries have been the last outposts of autoc-

racy. Our leaders speak of the confusion of youth. They
do not see the very definite confusion of the elders. Not
knowing what to do about many situations, they are not disposed to sit down and discuss them on the basis of equality
with those who could possibly enlighten them. Nor does it
dawn on many of them that they ought to do so. They are
products of the age in which orders were given and taken with
little questioning; an age which was comfortable for authority,
if not always productive. Authority now is in the situation of
the parents whose child, always docile and obedient, suddenly
appears intransigent. Somewhere they lost sight of the fact
that their "child" is now twenty-one, quite capable of voting
for the president or dying in Vietnam. These young people
are anxious for guidance and direction but they are intolerant
of unenlightened dictatorship, hiding its shortcomings behind
unconditional demands, its inadequate vision behind standards it did not meet itself, its uncertainty behind the loud
voice and harsh judgment.

Many a bishop has stated that the most important appointment in his diocese is that of the rector of the seminary. He
is right. And, since his greatest consideration presumably went
into the appointment, criticism of his appointee is criticism
of him. The rector, therefore, tends to enjoy a certain immunity from vocal criticism. But no rector or bishop can
afford the luxury of immunity from criticism. His work is too
important. Just as priests ought to be proud of a penchant for
unsparing criticism when it is honest and productive, so the
bishop ought to know that the highest form of flattery is the
willingness of his priests to tell him what they think. Immunity from criticism means only immunity from hearing
criticism. It is ever present, even though seldom heard by
those who need it most. In the "good old days" before the
"new breed" whose frankness is a virtue long out of style,
authority was criticized as much as it is today, if not more,
but it could seldom be challenged for it so seldom really

listened. When a rector stays above and beyond criticism it means only that he has a way of insulating himself from the information he desperately needs to do a good job. The super-tragedy occurs when the whole staff, except the academic mavericks and some incorrigibles of integrity who don't last too long on most seminary staffs, enjoys this immunity too. Most immunities from the realities of living precede disaster.

There is no machinery in seminaries for getting valid and necessary criticism to the one who needs it most. Further-more, the label "destructive," so arbitrarily and unjustly placed on criticism indispensible to progress, has been a defensive cover for inept management. There is no such thing as criticism without the destructive element in it. Yet such criticism can be quickly judged uncharitable and even sinful by the very parties being criticized justly and fairly. There is no way to estimate the cost to the Church, its progress, and to souls, of shutting off this source of vital information, de-velopment, and improvement.

Esteem for criticism is adult. Seminaries have often been described as places where they make boys out of men. The ounce of truth in this pound of cliché is that the attitude that little boys should be seen but not heard has prevailed in seminaries where seminarians have been treated as little boys. In the Church that "little boy" is still a little boy at thirty-five years of age and ten years after ordination, an age and time of life when business and commercial interests would be ex-pecting his most productive work. It is hardly surprising that such a priest rarely feels any obligation to direct souls or even qualify himself for doing so when he is eternally the young priest whose opinion is worthless to the chancery. Does a man suddenly become a spiritual director at 35, 45, or 55 years of age? Hardly. In fact, as long as the little-boy label is put on him in the seminary and he is not treated as an adult, and encouraged to think for himself, to stand on his two feet like a man, he surely is not likely to wake up some day as a priest and find himself qualified to guide others.

A great deal of time has been wasted in seminary education. Student after student has said so, without serious effort being made to establish whether it is so or not. The student rash enough to make such a statement where it could be heard was suspect, not only throughout his seminary course, but for many years in the priesthood. It was often recalled after ordination, if he got that far, that he was always a radical, that he always had too much to say. And this regardless of whether his speech originated from his desire to serve the Church or really expressed the truth.

The traditional seminary teaching has never permitted dialogue. Some professors are honest enough to admit that they do not want some smart student embarrassing them. But the standard explanation is that the students are there to learn, not to teach. The students are treated as if they are "Charley McCarthy's" with tape recorders in their heads. It is not surprising, then, that young priests come out of seminaries prepared to teach the laity without being questioned on anything they say. They unconsciously absorb this attitude in the seminaries, and those who question them appear to them to be questioning the Church. Fortunately for the Church, it is less and less possible for the priest's words to go unchallenged. Apart from the fact that almost all the old values are being challenged, and those which can stand the challenge will survive, educated people appreciate their obligation to challenge what is dubious or questionable. Their pride may make them challenge what they do not like but their intellectual integrity demands that they challenge what they cannot accept. The priest who will not be challenged is like the doctor who is offended by the patient who questions his judgment, even though the patient's life depends on that judgment. The patient has not only the right but also the duty to question, and to seek a second opinion, if and when it seems desirable. Only the proud, insecure, and incompetent resent having their opinions questioned.

People of integrity are always aware of their limitations and fallibility; they are eager to learn and, most of all, eager to avoid mistakes which could cause serious inconvenience or harm to others. The seminary professor who resents a student's questioning his opinion is showing far too much pride in a job calling for some humility. Furthermore, the best productions involve consultation with all who have something to contribute. The failure in the seminaries to accept the "new breed" for what they are, to give them not orders but leadership, efficacious direction to their ideas and energies — this failure is what has led to near revolt. History shows that few changes were ever made until they were forced on the administration. Insofar as the shortage of vocations is real and not due to wastefulness of priests and the inadequate use of the laity, that shortage is due largely to the failure of authority to meet the challenge of change.

Seminary discipline has so obviously failed to achieve its intended goal that few doubt its inadequacy. While pointing out some of those inadequacies may be flogging a dead horse, failure to see them and adjust has led many young men to the impossible conclusion that discipline should be thrown out in its entirety. Certainly many minds are intensely interested in the question of discipline and only the most intransigent have failed to respect the validity of criticism in this regard. Still it has not been wisdom, but sheer necessity, which has only now forced authority to come to grips with the problem of discipline and to make hitherto unacceptable adjustments.

All the imposed discipline in the world will not make a disciplined man. Man's glory or his disgrace is that he either disciplines himself or refuses to do so. In the business world few men who are neither stupid nor lazy find it hard to succeed. Yet all the brains and ability in the world are useless without the discipline indispensable to success. And discipline which is not self-imposed can never be called discipline in the true sense. It may be conformity, obsequious servility, dissemblance, acquiescence, laziness, or gutless passivity, but it is not discipline. When such people find themselves in a position where they need discipline, as they inevitably must, it simply is not there. Discipline underlies the practice of every virtue, for no one deliberately practices good acts habitually, which is what virtue entails, without discipline. This is why virtue of a high order is so rare among professional religious men or women. They are most often conformists. Nuns who have taken and kept the vow of chastity for many years are understandably frightened at the thought of putting that virtue to the test now demanded by active engagement in the apostolate. The thought of giving the nuns the freedom enjoyed by effective people in the world all but panics their superiors. They are rightly convinced that a very high toll will be taken. These good women have practiced claustration rather than chastity; they have been sheltered from the occasions for the practice of the virtue. They are like the many good women of the Victorian age who were good primarily because they were sheltered or kept under close observation. The discipline of the seminary has hardly prepared the priest-to-be for the tests he will face in a world ready to respect men who are good by choice and conviction, not through respect of person, intimidation, or conformity. The world today has more respect than ever for good people, and certainly far greater need of them. Nothing makes people good but virtue. Virtue is largely self-discipline. Discipline underlies the virtue of every responsible person. Responsibility is only developed in the climate of freedom. The climate of freedom until very recently was unknown in seminaries.

The academic formation in seminaries is seriously deficient. With the advent of worship in the vernacular, most of the

Latin will soon be gone. Who can guess the waste of time and reduced scope of learning attributable to the continued use of Latin texts? Nothing essential to the priesthood or its work was gained by the use of Latin texts. The bond of unity in the Latin language was largely wasted where the bond of charity was not already strong. However, in addition to doing away with Latin texts in seminaries, the courses should be adapted to those with less academic endowment who would be streamed into elective courses suitable to their potential. Just as the Church in America has passed up a great source of vocations by not having provided, until very recently, a single avenue for late vocations to the priesthood, so too the seminaries have been far too rigidly set against special training for competent people without the required academic background. The priesthood, like most businesses, has found that the brightest students academically are not necessarily the most productive.

A staggering thing about the seminaries is that they spend four to eight or more years educating a man for the essential work of a priest, to preach, teach, and minister. Much time and effort are spent with varying degrees of success on the learning required for preaching, but little or no time is spent on the art of preaching. Commercial enterprises will spare no expense in preparing sales staffs for their work. Seminaries are operated on such a restricted financial budget that they do not compare in importance with the construction work in the diocese. They have possibly the worst facilities in the country for the teaching of public speaking and selling. Politicians, salesmen, businessmen, and others will go to great lengths to qualify themselves for addressing the public, yet surely the priest has far greater need of this training because talking is his public life, it is his business. Even in those orders dedicated to preaching there is a dearth of men who can really get their message across. Granted that one cannot expect to make a Cardinal Newman of a deaf-mute, something can be done to improve the worst of speakers if sufficient means, time, and thought are put into the project.

Men engaged in religious formation or the work of the spiritual life often wonder at the lack of charity among professional religious. While many of them worry about the scandal coming from airing the wrongs of religious life in the public press, few see the greater scandal that this lack of charity itself is. Disillusionment has come to many religious. They begin to believe there is more charity in the world than among professionally dedicated people. However, this condition should be expected because charity is real love, and real love thrives only in freedom. Rigid and detailed control of people blights the birth and growth of charity.

The present confusion about obedience comes mainly from this background of rigid control. Bishops and superiors are very concerned about the rebelliousness of youth, and the refusal of the young priests to give their superiors the respect of former times. But the obedience of old did not often involve respect, and very seldom love. It was the sufficient and acceptable form of obedience that one simply did what one was told, regardless. Authority rarely recognized obedience as the supreme act of love. A child truly obeys his parents not when he is terrified of them but when he loves them. The fulfillment of conditions imposed on a terrified child can in no way be classified as obedience. Obedience is the virtue by which a person freely shows respect and love for his superiors and the authority they represent. It is perfect obedience only when it is gladly given, willingly given, freely given. It is obviously never gladly given when forced; and it is conformity, not obedience, when pressured, as it so often is by respect of persons or the consideration of one's own best interests. Tragically the superiors who have been most content with conformity have been those least able to inspire obedience. They are the ones who now deplore the conditions of freedom which expose their shortcomings and inadequacy as superiors, their incompetence as leaders.

When seminaries are good places run by good men producing good priests they will have waiting lists of candidates. Highly qualified people, real people, will flock around them like bees around honey. With every kind of advertising gimmick used in ruthless competition for people's interest and investment, the world is too sophisticated to want much but the real thing. And nowhere is this truer than in the field of religion, which is so vital to the development of man. The only really impressive thing in a seminary faculty is real charity, and the modern students are more discerning of it than they are given credit for. They are not impressed by spiritual talk from materialistic men. They are least of all impressed by bright men full of pride, by the Christian life in which Christ is irrelevant. Holiness has no longer the appeal that goodness has, for it is too easy to be mistaken in its identification. Too many reasonable facsimiles have passed for holiness. Goodness, on the other hand, makes its presence felt like fire. It is hard to mistake it for something else. And if a mistake is made it is not for long.

Perhaps nothing points out the past misdirection of spiritual training so clearly as the "good" person's conviction that he must not love anyone. Many religious feel guilty when they know they love someone, despite the fact that Christ insists they are guilty when they don't love. The subterfuge of liking but not loving is a ridiculous one. So is that of loving "people in general but no one in particular." One can only love this person, that, or the other one, each of whom has a name, is an individual, lovable for what he or she is and has. The eagerness of the professional religious to repudiate individual and personal love reveals a twisted mind to those who appreciate that Christianity's essence is love, human love, the only kind of love of which a man or woman is capable.

Certainly few seminaries have taught priests how to love

people, individual people. Yet if they have not done so they have missed the essential of Christianity. Consequently priests are ordained who are arrogant, proud, ambitious, nationalistic, race conscious, worldly, and progressive, but the real priest needs one thing only, to love. Without this power he may succeed at anything else but he will be an impressive failure in the priesthood of Jesus Christ. No seminary can make a silk purse of a sow's ear, but it can be more discerning, purposeful, and inspiring if the right people run it the right way. Nothing can dispense authority from the continuous pursuit of right ways, not under the threat of extinction, but in the best times with the best of candidates in the greatest numbers.

Chapter 4

Communications

POPE John XXIII referred to the "prophets of doom," to those who think that things are getting out of hand and worry about whether the unleashed forces of evil can really be held in check. The accelerated pace of progress inclines man to believe that he is heading pell-mell toward "the end." His shattered nerves do nothing to reassure him. Apart from the fact that as a man gets older he has an accumulated knowledge of the tragedies which have shaken him, communications today are such that he has not only the problems in his own home and nation to contend with, but breakfast with the whole world's problems leaning against the coffee pot on the table before him. With television actually going to war with the troops, and radio news desperate for any trifle to break the boredom of hour-to-hour newscasts, precious little of importance happens anywhere that does not intrude on modern man, and many people are employed to make trifles sound important. These intrusions build the ranks of the millions of escapists who, content with the nearest available pleasure, find reality unbearable and look desperately for every loophole in their responsibilities.

Yet communications are not pure curse. They have probably done more for progress in the world than any other factor. Despite all evidence to the contrary, the world is a better place than it ever was in which to live. The fact that man now knows more about the world only *seems* to make it worse. Who can guess the injustices and wrongs which were perpetrated in the secrecy of a world sheltered from the "big eye" of television? Christian teaching urges people to remember that God knows all the secrets of the heart, and that nothing escapes His eternal vigilance. This does not impress larceny-bound people, intent on their own small desires. But the fear they cannot feel for the vigilant eye of God they now have for the ubiquitous eye of the television news camera. Men in public office were never under more intense scrutiny. The exposure of malfeasance is a daily occurrence because of this roving public eye. This mechanical adjunct to the eye of the poorest and most illiterate man has promoted widespread knowledge of and interest in the conduct of public affairs. They are undoubtedly better conducted because of it.

Communications also represent a great step of man into the future. Yet the Church, so quick to bless with book and bell, is strangely reticent about really blessing them by reaching out to use them in her daily work. So quick and constant in their warnings to men to be aware of their accountability, Church authorities are strangely ill at ease when faced with their own accountability to men for their omissions. This is the great need in Church administration, the willingness to measure up to public scrutiny, which can both expose the badness of men and challenge them to the great goodness required to inspire and save the world. This is what mankind desperately needs to see in a Church which has publicly dared to espouse the truth, to call itself the champion of the truth in a world which does so much of its business in lies. After all, that world needs to believe in something too. It certainly can never believe in something as fearful of the truth as it is itself. When those in authority show real fear of the truth, which they tend to do when the diplomatic is equated with the apostolic, they abdicate leadership.

One eminent churchman, speaking one day about a meeting of the bishops, said to me rather pensively, "I did not quite know what to say. I thought the matter over and decided that I would simply tell the truth." Even he laughed when I replied, "That must have been a very difficult decision to make, Your Eminence." The wish that such anecdotes were untrue or at least exaggerations does not remove them from the record. Nor does the fact that they are not recorded remove them from history, or purify the actions of such as act them out.

Communications are admittedly vital, and so demand thoughtful attention and study everywhere. Their indispensability to man in his life and work and their intrinsic value in the universal betterment of conditions all around him force man to explore them in depth. The dullest intellect alive can see that the cost of letting happen what could have been prevented through the use of communications has been inestimable. Even men of negligible goodwill have valued communications in settling crises which would have damaged their interests or enterprises. Surely, then, men of peace and goodwill who are charged with the work of Christ should be the very first to esteem and employ them.

Communication involves the correct transmission of one's ideas to another, and the right understanding of the message by the recipient. It is now admitted that there can be no irredeemable crisis among people where the lines of communication remain open. It is also admitted in the Church that the great failure in the past has been the entire lack of communication in areas of vital importance in the administration. Nowhere is this truer than between bishops and priests, between the head office and the men on the road. In the world of religion, where the most important single need is for the bishops to recover the goodwill of their priests, communication between these groups has been negligible. Nor will all the arguments about the fineness of many bishops and their democratic regimes and self-effacing ways change the truth of the situation. Nor will all the urging in the last few years by responsible power change the fact that what is taking place is happening far too slowly, and much too late.

Communication is impossible between people with nothing in common. Naturally, then, the selection of bishops who are not in the common mold of priests does little for communication with their priests. And it is a fact that too many bishops have been selected who have very little in common with their priests. More will be said about this later, but the fact remains that any system, however good, has to be changed periodically if the best results are to accrue, if the inherent weaknesses in the system are not to develop to the point of danger. And the present system of naming bishops is long overdue for a change, for it has now made the episcopate outside of mission countries the most exclusive club in the world.

The bases of communication are exact expression and correct understanding, and these depend on a foundation of goodwill. Where there is no goodwill, of course, there is no desire to communicate, and the mechanics of communication are simply used to confuse and confound rather than to clarify. However, exact expression demands that those communicating must speak the same language. Assuming that the bishop and the priest are of the same racial origin and national background, in the older and more established nations the same language can be assumed. The language barrier there comes from the very different points of view. The one giving the orders and the one receiving them have points of view so different that they might as well be from different worlds. This is the origin of the father-son relationship between the bishop and the priest.

Now it is recognized that this paternal-filial relationship, if it ever was desirable, is so no longer. The bishop is in no sense a father to the priest. This relationship did not exist between the apostles. Nor did our Lord say anything to indicate that this paternalism was to characterize the relationship between subject and authority. He Himself chose the role of brother, friend. Paternalism is something which crept in for many known and unknown reasons. It has inevitably led to strife and schism wherever it has held sway. It has produced arrogance on the part of authority and intransigence on the part of the subject. It has led to autocratic self-will on the part of authority and childish irresponsibility on the part of the subject. It has done precious little to develop or increase charity.

While all authority comes from God, it is a presumptuous man indeed who claims for himself the place of God in the life of another without an immediate and eerie awareness of his own limitations. And while some think they can wield their authority effectively without much obligation to do so worthily, few subjects see God in authority exercised in ungodly ways. Despite every exhortation to respect the office when one cannot respect the man, the happiness and success of any administration in religion depends on the constant mindfulness by the one in authority of the God he represents. The man in authority who forgets this for a moment cannot speak the same language as those he rules. Consequently there will never be any communication between him and his people.

The subject for whom the very word "subject" is demeaning and revolting or humiliating clearly indicates his primary interest in himself and the small world of his own wishes. He thus must interpret in a paranoidal way every word and action of the one cursed with the power to rule. There can never be communication between them. Nothing authority says will be correctly understood, regardless of how honest the effort to represent the source of authority as humbly as possible.

It must be assumed that these are the extremes about which little can be done. There is the vast central area in which much can be done. There must be no delay in doing everything possible to get communications established, open, and moving freely. The problem here is to find people with something worth saying and the ability to say it, and others willing to listen and able to understand. The graces and favors lavished by God on His Church surely would have been more productive of inspiring leaders had they not been so frustrated by men of small stature. This is made evident by the fact that in an age when the Church is pleading for all possible help from its sons, there is little help forthcoming. Too many of those sons for too long were blessed for not having an original thought, for doing nothing that would upset the status quo. This climate naturally favored the vested interests which grew strong and encompassed their fiefdoms. Regardless of the sincerity of this present appeal for help, its very novelty limits its credibility. The superior who actually wants help from his subjects has first to convince them that he means what he says.

Yet even with the birth of new leadership, its growth and development, understanding (or, more truly, the lack of it) remains the bleakest area of progress in communication between authority and subject.

Successful communication depends more on understanding than on anything else. But what is understanding? It is the ability to comprehend what is apprehended. Yet it is often confused with agreement. One party in a dispute does not consider that the other understands unless he also agrees. Understanding is comprehension. There may also be agreement, but there is a great deal of difference between the two. More marriages get into trouble through lack of understanding than through lack of love. Yet for most people love means understanding; the two are identified, though they are very different. Love has little tolerance for lack of understanding which, like love, of its nature must be freely given, which like love can never be compelled. Genuine love cannot demand agreement; it can only hope for it. Even the most ardent love finds itself in trouble when it assumes that because the other person loves, he also understands, let alone that he also agrees. Under the demands for absolute agreement love withers and dies.

Just as the demand for agreement kills love, so does it kill communication. When a husband speaks and the wife understands, she simply comprehends what he is saying. She is not necessarily agreeing with him. But the fact remains that understanding people usually have harmony because understanding requires tolerance. Tolerance is the goodwill to see and appreciate a point of view contrary to one's own. Few knowledgeable churchmen will deny that this is the very thing which has been clogging the lines of communication between the bishops and their priests for generations. The few priests with opinions contrary to those of their bishops were intolerable. They were considered disrespectful, proud, rebellious, intransigent, and so on. Yet there was seldom a question of whether it might or might not be the bishops who were proud. Authority seemed to be set in an unassailable position. One could not question the bishop without questioning God, despite the very obvious distinction. Even today, in an age of a somewhat enlightened democracy, it comes as a shock to many in authority that they are questioned at all, or that they are made to account for their decisions, plans, or programs. It has been a dubious tribute to the docility of the clergy that this condition has persisted for so long. This dubious tribute largely explains the poverty of leadership, the sparing and modest use of talent presently evident in the Church.

In commending the children of this world, Christ seemed to indicate that they at least knew what was good for them, whereas the business of the Church seemed to suffer greatly from the administration of the children of light, so prone to consider themselves good because they intended to be good, right because they did not want to be wrong. The problem here is well illustrated by one father who often said that first he wanted to know *if* his children were thinking, and then he wanted to know *what* they were thinking. He could do neither of these things if he was not prepared to listen to them, which he was.

There has been far too little listening and even less understanding between the bishops and the priests. The first penalty to the Church is its poverty of leadership. Leaders simply cannot be developed in such conditions. The second, of course, is its poverty of program. When the flow of ideas is one way only, from the top down, the talents of the subjects are lost to the work. Such conditions led to the heartbreak of Pope Pius XI at the loss to the Church of the working classes. As far as the working man was concerned the messages from the top might as well have been coming from Mars. If these conditions persist there will be more and more losses, and the Church will be considered nearly irrelevant by a world so desperately in need of its potential spiritual leadership and gifts.

It is unusual, to say the least, when a studied effort is made to unearth these talents of priests and use them to capacity for the Church. The star of most priests rises according to their personal loyalty to the bishop, and their personal devotion to and work for him. Few question how men can be really loyal to other men in the true sense of the word, if they are not, first of all, loyal to Christ, God, and truth. In the aftermath of Vatican II many bishops are asking their priests to come forward with any ideas they have for the better development of the administration and work of the Church. These bishops are certainly to be commended for doing so. However, the fact remains that in most cases their priests simply do not believe they mean it, or, even more tragically, they are convinced that the bishops would reject out of hand most of the worthwhile expressions forwarded to them. In other words, there is a sort of impasse in the face of circumstances which though new to this generation are undoubtedly only one of history's repetitions. Other bishops in other times have asked for advice only to discard it without serious examination.

When opening the lines of communication which have been shut for years, tremendous tolerance is required of those not known for tolerance, if the flood of bitterness clogging those lines is to pour out in the clearing process. The silence of the past, which by authority was so readily misconstrued as agreement, would seem like heaven to those so long insulated from the clamor of revolt. Yet the clamor must not be closed off. It must be allowed to run its course while patience bears fruit in progress.

Two main factors militate against opening the long-closed lines of communication. One is the traditional silence which, enforced by sanctions, has been the very plug which closed the lines. The other factor is secrecy.

Secrecy has cloaked too many of the deliberations and decisions of an authority overanxious to maintain its aura of infallibility even in those areas in which it is not required. Perhaps in a church which had been so persecuted, secrecy became a second nature to its administration. Yet today, when all world authority is subject to a public scrutiny unequalled in history, undreamed of by numbers of people in the past, secrecy in its actions and deliberations makes the most respected authority suspect and the highest integrity dubious. Certainly it should never exist where it can possibly be avoided, and it should always be restricted to its minimal requirements. Secrecy is, after all, the antithesis of communication. And communication is the basis of trust. Secrecy, where it does not cloak that which cannot bear scrutiny, closes most avenues of help needed in the very situation considered serious enough for secrecy. Where it is so often used to sym-

bolize charity, it is more often a cover for irresponsibility or
ineptness. It fosters spiritual nepotism; it makes the best
appointments impossible or accidental. It dispenses from the
obligation to the future, from planning and provision. But
fundamentally, the tragedy of secrecy is that it cuts off the
head of the Church from the body, making an integrated, well-
functioning body impossible.

Few people have the personal integrity and zeal to live for
a long time deeply aware of their accountability to God. This
is tragically true of those so burdened with detailed administrative responsibility that they have little time to think of
their broader obligations. For this reason wide open and
efficient channels of communication between the bishops and
their priests should be set up and kept running. The purpose
of these channels should be the even two-way flow required
for true communication. In a Church where parental authority was equally blessed and stressed, it has been all too easy
to let all authority take on the qualities of parentalism. Special
effort has to be made to achieve and safeguard the adulthood
of subjects in any hierarchical order. Subjects are not children;
they do have rights and responsibilities. Superiors do have
obligations which their subjects must make them face, if
subjects are to faithfully serve God. Only in the last fifty
years, when life expectancy has increased so greatly, has the
dependence of parents on their children become so evident.
It is ridiculous for parents to anticipate respect from their
children when they themselves have no respect for their
Father, God. It is equally ridiculous for subjects to respect a
superior who has little or no respect for truth.

Living and working in the age of democracy, the Church
can ill afford to lag behind in setting up the channels of communication required by democracy. Paternalism in the Church
has not disposed it to accept even the ideals of democracy
which are feasible and good. Democracy requires the administration of authority in a way that is at once responsible and

effective. The Church, jealous of its authority, has taken its power to punish very seriously. But any willingness to punish should be matched by an equal willingness to be held accountable. Without this balance, authority flutters between overanxiousness to correct and overfearfulness of being wrong. Nothing but good can come to the Church and souls by communication and dialogue which establish and maintain a healthy interdependence between authority and subject.

Such channels would also bring the Church up to date corporately. There is no successful organization in the free world today in which the decisions are the work of a single mind, of one individual. To look upon corporate decisions as a violation or weakening of personal authority rather than a safeguard for its better administration is deception. The trend to corporate decision has come, not from a world in which genius is no longer rare, but from a world in which educated thinkers are plentiful and available. The world's decisions are of such seriousness that they require the combined ideas and contributions of all available talent. Teilhard de Chardin called this trend to corporate decisions an indication of "man's irreversible rise to the personal." This world, rather than becoming more impersonal, and people becoming just small cogs in great machines, is becoming, according to him, more personal with far more individuals involved in the decisions made for the people. These decisions can be far better, with far happier consequences, than so many of the decisions of history which were made impulsively by men of power rather than of talent, and for their personal satisfaction rather than for the common good.

The overcautious have, for years and years, been preaching the dangers of socialism. Yet it was largely their intransigence, in the face of obligations unacceptable to them, which brought into being the socialism we have today. When man cannot be called upon to fulfill his obligations in charity, he will be compelled to do so by law, even though that law is socialistic in the general sense of the word. And this obligation is now canonized by the Church in its exhortation to men and nations to share this world's goods. Those who need them may not always deserve them, but as children of God they have equal rights with those who have been more fortunate or worked harder for them with their God-given talents. The breeding and rearing which developed the talents of the latter for hard work and productivity were not earned either, but were the free gifts of God.

Regardless of the complaints against authority for its failure to set up and use communications, the priests are generally children of their fathers and have been guilty of the same thing in relation to the people. There has been, certainly, as little communication between priests and people as there has been between bishops and priests. The consequences of this are being met belatedly, with as much grace as possible, by priests who were admittedly too slow in seeing them come.

Just as parentalism has been the pattern of episcopal authority, so has paternalism been the pattern of the relationship between the priest and the people. This has been natural enough to a point, for in a world largely unlettered and uneducated the priest was much more a leader than the average person. The situation was paralleled a few years ago by the position or role of the local physician whose advice to his patients was seldom restricted to their physical ills and the general condition of their bodies. He was an educated man whose opinion was respected and sought. And although he gave out much advice he was not qualified to give, his advice was respected by people less qualified than he. The same could be said of the local teacher or lawyer. However, universal education has made this pseudo-omniscience obsolete. In fact, medical men now are so aware of their limitations that they seldom give advice in any area of medicine which is not their specialty.

Times have changed and the ignorant and unlettered people who were the recipients of the charity and interest of the clergy are fewer. Most people are educated, able and willing to return to the clergy some of their time, talent, and possessions. The clergy must not be too proud to take their gifts. The clergy insisted on and provided education for the poverty-stricken and illiterate immigrant. That immigrant, three generations later, is an educated man, and yet the administration of the Church acts toward him as if he were still wallowing in ignorance. The Church is failing to meet the challenge of its own success, not distinguishing between those anxious to work with it and those who would revolt against it. It must move quickly to find fruitful use for those who are so willing and able to shoulder the burdens of their faith. It must reject the role of the parent who lavishes everything on the child and then is disappointed when the child no longer has a desperate need of him. It must rejoice when the child is successful in his own right. In other words, parentalism or paternalism is finished in the Church of America, everywhere except in its work among the Negroes whom in the past it had been willing to leave as orphans. And not for long will paternalism be needed in the work among the Negroes. They will make much quicker progress than the white immigrants because the climate and facilities are ready for it now.

The term "people of God" as a new name for the Church connotes only the fact of the adulthood of the laity, of the passing of the conduct of the Church from the hands of the clergy to the hands of all the people including the clergy. The bishops and clergy have been the Church in our day. As one bishop erroneously put it to one of his priests, "I am Canon Law in this diocese." Now they are no longer the Church but an essential part of it, one essential part among other essential parts. The hierarchical Church has meant a dictatorial Church both in the good sense of a benevolent dictatorship and the bad sense of tyrannical paternalism. Both qualities dispensed the Church from communicating much important Christian teaching. One of the manifest results of this dispensation is the Catholic who had his conscience formed for him by the theologians rather than having had their help in forming his own conscience. This man developed behavior patterns so constant as to be called principles. Under the seige of modern living these "principles" proved to be mere conformity never formed into personal convictions.

The whole birth-control controversy further illustrates this weakness. The people, as well as the clergy, now realize that Catholics were simply told what was a mortal sin and what a venial one. And despite the fact that they were also taught that to commit a mortal sin they had to have serious matter, full knowledge, and full consent, they accepted the classifications of sins as given them. Few ever explored what full knowledge and full consent entailed. It was presumed that the full understanding of and willingness to perform the act, regardless of the severity of the pressures involved, were enough to determine some action in itself to be a mortal sin. And this despite the sinner. This indicated a very great weakness in communication, in teaching, which is the essential work of the Church. And this mistake was made because the priests did not consider the real need to convince the people by explanation but only the need to tell them by instruction and decree.

No good teacher finishes a lesson and still leaves the students uninformed. Yet this has been the pattern of teaching from Catholic pulpits. It has led to the countless number of good people of some integrity who have left the Church because of this "you sinned because we say you sinned" Catholicity. They could no longer see the point of going to Mass every Sunday "if they were cut off from grace"; if they could not receive the sacraments just because they were told something in which they knew they lacked full will was a mortal sin, just because the priest said it was. They were taught that the priest was a judge in confession rather than that he was there to hear the judgment they had passed on themselves, and forgive them in the name of God who alone was capable of real judgment.

The priests have been seriously at fault in their inability to communicate publicly in their sermons. They have been far more at fault in their inability to communicate privately with their people. Apart from the fact that it has been almost a spiritual maxim that the priest should not mix with the laity, there has been remarkably little availability of the priest to the people in their personal needs. Thoughtful people today are getting a great deal of help from professional counselors which they should have been able to get from their priests. Of course, counseling by priests has been restricted almost exclusively to the confessional, even though confession is neither the time nor place for counseling. There the very desirable anonymity militated against the best results. The confessional made physical discomfort and the public manifestation of one's problems inevitable, even when the priest was qualified to counsel and had the time and patience to do so. Confessions are seldom heard at the convenience of the people, and those needing the most help seldom get it at the times appointed for confession because of the large numbers seeking only absolution. Confessions should be held at the convenience of the people and competent well-trained priests should be available for counseling by appointment.

As for private counseling, most priests have not been prepared for this apostolate, nor have they developed the understanding or wisdom required for good judgment. Nor do they, with all the minor chores of less importance to be done, acquire the experience for counseling which is not a sideline but an essential phase of priestly work.

Where there is a difficulty in communication it is hard to escape the conclusion that there is really little prayer or ability to pray. For prayer, which ought to be the heart and center

of priestly life, is nothing more than communication with
God. It is a fact that, regardless of the time a priest spends at
prayer, he is not necessarily communicating with God. He
may be only thoroughly engrossed in self, and preoccupied
with the problems of self, which seldom have much to do
with God directly, but are, apart from God, without solution.
The challenge to the Church has always been to communicate. The apostles were charged by Christ to go forth and
communicate to the world all the things they had seen and
heard. But at no time has the challenge been greater, nor
have the means to meet that challenge been more numerous
so sophisticated through exposure to the world's greatest
so sophisticated through exposure to the world's greatest
orators on radio and television that the average dull Sunday
sermon is tuned out pretty quickly; this exposure too has
given the people a greater appetite for worthwhile things. It
is, therefore, a great pity that all priests are not better preachers. Electronic devices and aids make it possible for the worst
speaker to be heard, if only he would do his part and have
something worth hearing. Again, it has never been more
possible to present the best speakers to more people than
now through mass communication systems. But whereas
artists, comedians, and performers of all kinds are competing
for the airwaves which represent personal success and prosperity to them, the Church has made but meager efforts to
develop its performers, or to get the ablest preachers of religion before the largest numbers. In fact, the single man who,
despite envy and much criticism, has made a great name for
himself, did so virtually on his own by sheer effort, dedication,
and the hard pursuit of excellence. There must be a hundred
like him in America, but who has sought them out or set
them on the way?

The Church as a monitor of public morals has been far
more apt to condemn than to provide. The world today is
simply not interested in waiting around to have its lives and

works censured. But it will be led to great things by those who have an interesting and workable program to offer. Those prophets of doom who say that the people are just not interested in the better things of life are blind to evidence all over the country of the eagerness of people for adult education, opportunities for retraining and acquiring better qualifications for work. If they are not interested in religion, it is largely because it is presented to them badly. Religion appears to them as irrelevant, as involving a questionable set of standards not obviously improving those accepting them, and not of much help to those who need an answer now.

Despite the fact that a world without religion is as badly off as a man without a job, this has not been made evident. The people do not need the trappings of religion but they need the heart of religion which is Jesus Christ, God. Organized religion has been so busy with its organization that a person can call himself a Christian today without believing or perhaps even considering that the measure of his Christianity is the degree of his likeness to Christ. And there are innumerable arguments to support the fact that even religious men and women feel little compulsion to act and live like Christ.

By far the best vehicle of communication is happiness. Everyone in the world wants it. No one ever knocks it. And where there is happiness it is communicated; indeed, by its very nature it communicates itself. No Madison Avenue adwriter need present it attractively to a world already interested. But where happiness does not exist no amount of subterfuge can make the searchers see it. Religion is the greatest source of peace and happiness in the world. Religion which does not bring peace and happiness is false. If true religion does not bring peace and happiness to a world hungry for them, it is for lack of happy Christians. Somewhere the lines of communication are blocked, and they can only be blocked by selfishness, as obvious and very understandable reasons would indicate.

The challenge to communicate what the Church has to offer seems presently to have surpassed the ingenuity of those whose business is to get it across. That is an unnecessary pity. Those who should do it, apparently cannot, and those who can do it are not being permitted to do so. The proudest people find it hard to accept the success of others. Their failure is never so obvious as when they prevent others from succeeding. Yet, when the main effort goes to keeping others down there is less for everyone. No nation has learned this a harder way than Soviet Russia. In a world that needs commodities all the time, there is no room for the exclusion of the capable from productivity. There is room only for expansiveness. Surely charity is nothing if not this. And the Church is nothing if it has not charity. When the Church has little but empty words to communicate, men, not God, have made it so. And the Church has left many good things unsaid because those in authority were not the ones who thought of them.

Chapter 5

Reorganization of the Administration

SOCIALISM was quite roundly condemned in the famous *Syllabus of Errors* of Pope Pius IX. It got the treatment, there and then, that atheistic Communism got in the first half of the twentieth century. Yet today the word *socialism*, while still opprobrious to the ultraconservative right, has an almost diametrically opposite meaning. Blessed with a new name and called socialization, it has been praised and recommended by Pope John XXIII. Many would like to believe that the Church has changed its teaching, for then its authority could be questioned. The change is in the meaning and understanding of words rather than in teaching. Those who used to say "up in the sky," in view of new discoveries and new knowledge, now more correctly say "out in space." Public responsibility has come to have a different meaning and a different acceptance. In the face of geographic, economic, and political changes in the intervening years, private ownership has not been repudiated so much as the right attribution has been made of all things to God whose will it is that they be shared. Christians with this world's goods must share with those without them.

Few words fail to change their significance with time and

use. Even when the significance itself is not changed, the concept involves a great deal more than previously. So it is with the word *administration*. Administration today connotes a managerial method, activity, and efficiency not conceived of in other days. The concept of industry, which was portrayed by clanging machinery powered by sooty, coal-fed furnaces belching the black smoke shrouding slum neighborhoods where the slaves of industry lived in squalor and ill-health, is in no way comparable to the modern image of spotless factories electrically powering automated production lines supervised by educated, cleanly-smocked blue-collar workers. Yet nowhere in America today can any but the latter type of factory be established. Apart from its intolerable ugliness the former type is quite uneconomical. The beautiful lawns of industrial sites in zoned areas are more carefully manicured than many in residential areas. So, too, administration in the Church should not only be modern, but it should be administration in the marvelously progressive and technically productive sense, first-class administration. The administration which fails to change and modernize decides its own fate. It will be left so far behind that it could only be hopelessly inadequate and wasteful.

The administration of the Church needs such changes. This is admitted by all, right up to the Pope and Council. How to make these changes is the challenge.

There are three main obstacles to the early and radical change required in Church administration. First, the conservatives in charge lack the vision and are immune to pressure on themselves. Second, there is little awareness in depth of the urgency and desirability of utilizing modern technological facilities. There is both inertia, resisting change, and little grasp of the tremendous possibilities of converting such facilities to apostolic use. Third, there is conservatism, bordering on miserliness, in using Church money for productive efficiency rather than for basic necessity. The funds are there for this purpose, if they are not hoarded through undue caution and a peculiar sense of private ownership by the administrators. The knowhow is also there. The faithful, always generous in the face of worthy causes, will be supergenerous in a matter of such advantage to themselves, and at such testimony of the administration's respect and solicitude for the people of God.

The organizaton of the Church, especially on the diocesan level, is geared to management rather than to the requirements of the apostolate. Now it must be geared to the apostolate. No longer is the work of the Church to be measured in territory to be traveled and buildings to be erected, but in minds and hearts to be won and guided. At the turn of the century, materials were the main consideration in building and labor costs were negligible; now the situation has reversed itself. In the missionary days of the Church the rigors of travel and survival were the main considerations and the work was secondary to just being there; now travel and survival are easy, and the work to be done is paramount. In the early days of the Church, money, buildings, and providing and expanding material facilities were of primary importance. Now the provision of highly qualified personnel and personal competence in exacting fields of work are the main issues. It is not that the material facilities are to be minimized, but rather that the work done with them alone can justify or bless them in the name of Christ.

There is a strikingly parallel situation in medicine. The failure to read the signs of the times in the medical profession has brought things to a critical pass. At a time when the government is about to provide free medical care for all (if one can call free what is paid for with taxes and assessments of various kinds), the great difficulty to be faced is the lack of medical personnel required for such services. Whereas previous financial drives emphasized the costs of buildings and facilities, now second-thinking makes it plain that unless

sufficient personnel is going to be forthcoming, that is, young
people of better intelligence willing to spend many years
qualifying themselves through study and hard work, Medicare
will be a hollow joke. And it is becoming more and more
obvious that one simply cannot take a young person of high
intelligence and eagerness for success and make a public
servant of him. He will undertake his life's work in some
field more personally rewarding. Even Russia has learned, the
hard way, the value and indispensability of incentives.

The administration of the Church is facing a problem
equally acute and serious, with many of the same factors
involved. This must be quickly recognized while there are
still young people willing to make themselves available to the
Church and its work. Those in authority are not just alarmed at
the dearth of vocations; the mortality rate among those
already in the work of the Church has them equally disturbed.
The second-thinking which would have come from real
humility is now made inevitable by sheer necessity. The
young people are simply not inspired by the caprice of an
unrealistic administration lacking the commitment demanded
by the gospel. There is no such thing as escape from accountability by pleading the dignity of either person or office.
People are more and more aware that they themselves are
the Church. Like stockholders in a corporation, they want to
know how things are being handled. People today want to
know what they are getting into before they buy or contribute.
They want answers and they want truthful answers fearlessly
and gladly given for the sake of what is involved. This the
administration must face, or betray the cause of Christ and
Church through pride and presumption. The Church can no
longer be run like the back forty acres of the old homestead,
or thought of as "my" diocese by the bishop.

The acceptable philosophy of the free world today is democratic with all of democracy's inherent good and bad points.
The Church cannot sit back and say that it is not a democracy

but a hierarchical institution. The ways of its personnel are going to be democratic or it is going into discard. Who needs more proof that the road of history's passing is littered with casualties, the procrastinators, the sightless leaders of the blind, the isolated tyrants, and the diehard conservatives with neither the interest, capacity, nor compelling necessity to keep abreast of the times? Those who hold for the irreconcilability of a hierarchical institution with democracy are not realists; they are just too comfortable in the status quo. They are usually the vested interests. That there are such interests in the Church is evidence that the Church is a human institution; its divinity consists only in its establishment by Christ and the continued presence of its founder within it. The problem is not one of the nature of the Church or the principles involved in authority and obedience, but rather the identification of the best interests of the Church with those of the people of God. Important decisions are to be made and essential work for humanity is to be done. Unquestionably, the more highly qualified people motivated by zeal and the love of God who are involved in the direction of things in the Church, the better will be the work of the Church and the greater the good done. The job is to take the steps necessary to assure that these people are ready and put to work, not by whimsy but by design, not by accident but by plan.

This job can never be done when, in response to any complaint or suggestion, the ideal is pointed out as the real, and the teaching of the Church quoted rather than the current situation faced. The weaknesses of the existing administration are not only to be admitted but to be earnestly sought out and remedied. Nor is that charity impressive which urges the very tolerance and understanding for the administration which has not been very evident in the administration's handling of the people of God. For example, those religious who heard the glories of docility and obedience extolled with ceaseless and unstinting praise by their superiors now stand waiting for their superiors to show such docility and obedience to the decrees of the Council and the expressed wishes of the Holy Father. And many of them stand waiting in vain.

Because the Church administration is oriented to management rather than the apostolate, quite naturally and even reasonably, the problems of the Church are handled from the management point of view rather than the point of view of the people of God. The people continue to suffer from the ill-advised decisions and acts of the management and the weaknesses of the administration. It has been all but forgotten in practice that, according to Christian teaching, whatever is done or omitted for one of these least brethren is done or omitted for Jesus Christ. It is because of this orientation that there are many complaints against celibacy. Sexual morality and marriage regulations, it is said, are handled from the point of view of the celibate for whom many aspects of these areas have little or no personal relevance. Then again, when management gets top-heavy and is continually obsessed with the respect due it regardless of its dedication or effectiveness, it is very reasonable for the people to ask if Jesus Christ is really important to the management of the Church. The asking of this question, without getting a reasoned and dispassionate answer, has indicated a callous indifference to souls, and has led to the disenchantment of many with the Church. Surely, if the individual has no appeal against injustice in the Church of the just God, people are going to throw up their hands in disbelief. They will tend to charges of hypocrisy against the Church on the one hand or to active antagonism on the other. The reason many people hate the Church is not so much because of its human weaknesses, which they easily understand and accept, but because of the insistence in its own case that this human weakness really represents God and cannot be dealt with without questioning the very authority of God. This insistence is intolerable to the man of integrity and a terrible incitement to the vicious man eager to excuse himself for almost any rebellious act. Many who insist that "God is dead" are confusing God with those men of God among the living dead, authorities using God for their own honor and glory, for the preservation of their legal prerogatives.

Unless the Church in its management makes provision for the hearing and expeditious handling of the problems of individual people, all its talk about loving the poor and doing the work of Christ, the shepherd of souls, becomes idle and a mockery of the great spiritual reality of God's fatherhood. This has been a basic and serious problem in the history of the Church. In fact, despite the Church's teaching that it exists for the good of the individual, which is quite contrary to the Communist teaching that the individual exists for the good of the state, the actual practices of both regimes have been too often alike for the comfort of honest men. The reduction of the secular arm of the Church to the Swiss Guard was a happy event. With the loss of temporal power, the growth of the Church had to depend on the goodwill of individuals rather than on the strong arm of the Catholic powers aligning themselves with God for their own advantage.

Nowhere has the Church's orientation to management been more evident than in the handling of souls. For example, a priest resident in Rome itself, and in good standing, simply could not get the faculties to hear the confession of a fellow priest. Possession and use of the faculties to hear confessions in cases of necessity depend more on legal technicalities than on the needs of the souls in question. Why should not any priest in good standing, possessing the faculties in his own diocese or the place to which he is attached, be able to hear the confession of someone in need, anywhere? No matter how much the argument is brought forward that the sacraments must be safeguarded, this is belied by the prodigality of the death of Christ for man and the failure of Christ to safeguard Himself from the dangers involved in living with sinners. Far more care is taken in safeguarding the sacrament of penance than in safeguarding the sacraments of baptism, confirmation, Holy Eucharist, or matrimony. But in any case, the sacraments are for men and must be exposed to misuse as are all men's servants, although he sins who uses them abusively. Authorities have been accustomed to considering the problems of the Church as "their" personal problems. "Maintain the law" has been canonized because the law is heavily weighted in favor of the administration rather than the people.

The fact remains, above and beyond all management problems, that Christ did say, "Think you first of the things of the kingdom of heaven and all other things will be added unto you." It requires highly qualified Scripture scholars to mull over the meaning of Holy Writ and come up with erudite answers, but Christ's words were spoken to the ordinary man to be understood by him and related to himself and his life in the world. If the Church administration is like Christ and His words oriented to that man, then it will be run well. If it is not, it will be a big business management insofar as it is effective, and a privately run enclave insofar as it is not. As has already been said, it was a matter of great pride to many Catholics that an important business management concern from America made a detailed appraisal of the Vatican and its management of the affairs of the Church, and came up with the information that the management was in a very superior class, nearly equal to that of the world's best. Whether or not you deny the validity of the appraisal, there is no real basis for comparison except one which can lead to deception and complacency. A realistic look at the world to which the Church has been sent plainly indicates that its management is wasting time congratulating itself. Chanceries should be incentive centers rather than restrictive forces. They should be there to inspire and help, and in rare cases where authority's delusions of grandeur are minimal, they are.

The famous principle of canon law perhaps puts it best when it says, "Favorable things are to be taken in their broadest sense, odious things in their most restricted sense." But it is the most ignored principle in practice. It is never used where authority is jealous of its prerogatives, and it can never be used by people where personal judgment is restricted.

The decree On The Church in the Modern World clearly states in its introductory paragraphs that "It [the Church] is inspired by no earthly ambition," but the realist will immediately dismiss this as an evasion. The management of the Church is filled with men and forces with great earthly ambition. The zeal of otherwise dedicated men for the good of the Church too often appears to be zeal for power to command the world and have it obey, not the basic commands of Jesus Christ, but the organizational statutes of the establishment.

It is not sufficient to say, in reply to critics, that the Church is run by human beings with all the weaknesses of human beings. This is all too evident. The world is waiting with shortened patience for some evidence that the so-called dedicated men who run the Church do try harder to be good, to be just, to be honorable. Although it was clearly pointed out in the Council that the Fathers must admit their failures and weaknesses before the world, it was much to the chagrin of many of the Fathers that it was admitted before the whole world that they had sinned, and that the Church had failed its mission, at many times and in many places in history. Arrogance and pride seldom sit well with authority of any kind, at any time. But they surely are most unfitting in that authority claiming its power from Christ, who, being God, humbled Himself and thought it not beneath Him to be crucified. Nothing can possibly explain to a cynical world the abuse of charity in a Church which claims charity as its fundamental principle. And the administration of the Church, however legal it may have to be, must have that charity which begins at home as its beginning, end, and purpose. Nor can any time be lost in getting on with this orientation in a world traveling as fast as this one seems to be toward a day of reckoning.

The commonest description of youth today is that it is involved in an obvious and anxious search for personal identity. Soon it will be too late for the individual search for identity; humanity itself will be searching for an identity. The Church has the answer. Of that there can be no doubt. But that answer is all but obscured by the failure of the Church, until just now, to identify itself with the people. The zeal of management for the development of the Church and its power over men has done nothing to convince the people that they are the Church, rather than its servants. It is very difficult to reconcile the unmistakable conditions of Christ for forgiveness of sin, "as we forgive those who trespass against us," with the legalistic approach to salvation and justifiication used by the management of the Church today. But this reconciliation is not beyond the men whose job it is to meet the challenge. Only the time factor seems threatening. It is running out rather quickly.

The prime factor involved in the reorganization of the administration should be the establishment of the Church as the spiritual force in the lives of men. Therefore its developmental and expansive aspect rather than its punitive aspect should predominate. To assure this being done the Church must be mined for the talented people needed to direct the positive reconstruction and reorientation. Emphasis should be on the advance rather than the safeguard, without, of course, commending folly. Needless to say, the first step in the program, if the suggestion will bear continued repetition, is to assure that the appointment of bishops will no longer depend on the present system. It is true that any system of appointing bishops will have personal and political overtones, but there must be more objective ways of seeking out talent, competence, and dedication. The people of God desperately need better leadership. Ways of getting it must have top priority. Certainly computers should not be excluded in this matter, nor should the human mind with its vagaries, subjectivity, and self-interest be retained as the only basis for selection. Wisdom, after all, is nothing more than a personal data-processing system. The computer, modeled after this system, has the advantage of operating without interference by the emotions, without prejudice for or against, giving one man the benefit of many men's experience.

In lieu of the discovery of better ways and means, many new ways should be tried. These ways will have built-in flaws but they cannot be delayed much longer, for the flaws of the present system compound each other. The popular election of bishops has something to offer, since the people of God are better educated, and the appointment of the shepherds is the work of the Church. Such a way is frowned upon, but is no more objectionable than having governments propose suitable candidates for the approval of the Vatican. There is nothing contradictory about admitting human ways into a church of divine origin. In a world where industry never tires of searching out new ways of making money the Church should not tire of searching out new ways of making its representation more effective. This is not done when the administration is dispensed from charity by the requirements of legal structures. When such things as the appointment of shepherds can be handled in a way in which the best candidates by far can be overlooked or bypassed, serious reorganization is desperately needed.

Better reorganization of the administration will always be impossible while authority denies its necessity. It will be easy enough to improve the system if the necessity is admitted. But let it be admitted while there is still a body of believers to shepherd. Or must we be convinced again only in restrospect that something should have been done because we now see the calamitous effects of its omission?

Chapter 6

Priests and Parish Work

IF THE pope and the bishops are running the head office, the priests are the salesmen on the road. Any modestly successful business enterprise makes clear that much depends on the effective channels between the head office and the men on the road. Every company representative should have all the authority, freedom of plan, and scope for judgment that the best interests of the business permit and the good judgment of the representative makes possible. Anything more than this lets things get out of hand, and anything less causes the arteries of the business to clog, harden, and deteriorate.

The one thing which makes a priest effective at the parish level is his spirituality. It is the reason for the priest's presence in the parish. He is to give the parish its spiritual flavor. He is to sharpen the spiritual appetite of his people, to satisfy their spiritual needs to the greatest possible extent. He is to convince the people that they have here no lasting city, that they must lay up treasure where neither rust nor the moth consumes nor the thief breaks in and steals. In fine, he is to do everything to make God a reality in the lives of his people, to make them think first of the kingdom of heaven, so that all other things will be added unto them.

Obviously, then, the priest must be a spiritual man. And if he is not, his people have every reason to be let down, disappointed, for this, regardless of all his other talents, is the one thing they feel and believe they have a right to expect of him. But they may expect him to be so spiritual that he would have to be disembodied to fulfill their expectations. They may resent, to some degree, the full humanity which must be his if he is a man at all. What, then, constitutes a spiritual man? What do the people of God have a right to expect of their priests?

The answer to this is very simple indeed. It is, in fact, the very simplicity of the answer which makes it so difficult to grasp. A spiritual man is a man who has charity. Charity is love, and God is charity. A spiritual man, therefore, is one in whom God dwells. St. Paul says that the man without charity has nothing. Therefore, the priest without real love in his heart has nothing. The problem is love, real love. But what is love? Well, whatever it is, it is what a priest needs if he is to be a real priest, if he is to be to his people what they want him to be, what they need him to be. It certainly has not always been the expected requirement of the spiritual priest. Strangely enough, charity is at once too easy and too hard a thing for the man who would be spiritual. It is too easy because nothing can keep it from him but himself; it is too hard because there are so many facsimiles of it and so many distractions from it.

Because of the traditional and monastic approach to spirituality, the spiritual man is often considered the man of prayer. That is not to say the man who prays always, but rather the man who spends long hours at praying. Yet, very often the man who spends the most time at prayer is the man who seeks his own perfection rather than the will and work of God. The man of penance and mortification has often been considered the spiritual man. He is the man who goes around sad-faced and abstemious, not only denying himself all worldly pleasures but doing it obviously. To him, anything enjoyable has something wrong about it. Pleasure is suspect, somehow unworthy of God. These qualities make him look "good" to a pleasure-seeking world, but this man may not be really good. For seldom is the man really good who denies, rather than fulfills, himself in the right way, with the right things. Such a man may fit the traditional pattern of the spiritual man, but he can be without charity, and therefore nothing.

The best penance is that required by the fulfillment of one's duties and state in life. There is certainly nothing negative about this. But most people do not recognize this for the penance that it is. Penance is still, for most, going about with a long face, covered with metaphorical ashes, singing a dirge, complaining about the badness of people and the wickedness of the world. The man of charity exudes joy, exudes God, because God is dwelling in his heart. God is the gift he brings to his people. The unhappiness of others disturbs the priest of charity because he sees it as so unnecessary. He knows unhappiness to be the absence of goodness in people, the absence of God in their lives. The spiritual priest knows that it is not hard to have God in one's heart, mainly because God wishes to be in the hearts of men. The difficulty is to drive out the self which impedes, or makes impossible, the presence of God.

Few priests who really want to be good are unaware of the Blessed Sacrament in the church, and the sacramental presence of Jesus Christ in the Blessed Sacrament. In fact, the priest making any real effort to be good knows that he must spend time before the Blessed Sacrament. However, can the priest who appreciates this true presence and yet remains unaware of the true presence of Christ in his office, with the people coming to him for counseling and instruction, lay a claim to spirituality? Can the priest for whom God means everything, and in fact is his whole life, remain long unaware that wherever two or three are gathered to-gether in His name, there Christ is in their midst? Can he long remain unaware that the man at the door, the man in need, the poor and the neglected, are Jesus Christ? Yet what can these people really mean to the average priest when even the foreign missions of the Church, the work of Christ among pagans, draws little or none of his personal time, thought, or resources? Any and all objections notwithstanding, this unawareness, this disinterest, quite correctly gauges the spiri-tuality of the average priest. And if it seems to set the mark pretty low, it is just that way, regardless of charges of hang-ing him on a technicality of making one phase of Christ's work the whole work, of writing off his many other good qualities and activities as being of little or no consequence.

This is the priest today, where he stands, as he stands. And if Christ is not obviously with him in the office, in the pagan on the other side of the world as well as the poor in his own parish, that man is simply not a truly spiritual man. He is not a pastor in the sense that he is not actually invested in the work of Jesus Christ, the care of souls. He may be a competent executive, a man of edifying life; he may be with-out reproach among his neighbors; but he is a citizen of this world before he is a shepherd of Jesus Christ. Nothing he can say or do in his own justification can prove otherwise. And the people of God need spiritual men, men of God, good pastors.

Needless to say, the Mass is the mainstay of the spirituality of the priest. And again, the simplicity of the explanation almost seems to destroy its validity as an answer. When the priest goes to the altar he gives his life to the Father through Christ. When he comes away from the altar he should some-how or other be aware that he is no longer his own man but God's. So the things of God are paramount in his life. The so-called realist who tries to evade this spiritual truth is in actual fact an escapist. Every parable of Christ about stew-

ardship insists on this point. There is delusion in the gift
of one's life to Christ in the priesthood except where there
is reality in living that gift. The failure to so live is, of course,
the main explanation of unhappiness in the priesthood.
Those who scoff at this, and in the name of realism insist
that no one is capable of giving himself entirely to God, are
the very ones who so lack realism in the face of the extravagant praise given them on the occasions of ordination, or a
jubilee celebration, or the receiving of empty honors. The
priest to whom empty honors mean so much is the first to
deny the possibility of meeting Christ's challenge to total
dedication, or commitment, or whatever other current term
is used to describe the gift of oneself and one's life to God
through His grace. Nothing should be so resented by those
who believe in, love, and wish to serve Christ, as implying
such an impossibility. The spiritual priest, the man of charity,
is far too objective to see empty honors for anything but
what they are.

Though very few priests will be required to die on a cross
for their people, all of them have been called to live on a
cross for them. It is primarily through the actual gift of
himself daily to Christ through the Mass that the priest will
be made aware of the true specifications of his life and be
inspired to meet its requirements. If there is this daily offering, those priests bursting with enthusiasm for the new liturgy
will have some of that enthusiasm left over for the life that
is called for in the liturgy. If the "Gungho" vernacularists
are as interested in the Christian change of heart as they
are in the change of the language of worship, their worship
will be magnificent. If not, the appetite for change will represent the need for novelty, excitement of some kind, rather
than enthusiasm for Christ, the center of Christianity. The
appreciation of this truth is the barometer of spirituality. For
this is nothing more nor less than charity, the willingness to
carry the cross behind Christ, the acceptance of his role

among men today. Such a priest is no more than a good shepherd to his flock. All the fine deception of pseudosanctity, perfection, or holiness cannot change the fact that real priestly spirituality demands neither more nor less than being a good pastor. Anything else is a departure from Sacred Scripture and has no real basis in the Christian way of life.

To a good shepherd, the reality of Christ in the man he is dealing with at the moment is inescapable. It is not just material for a flowery panegyric at his jubilee or an extravagant eulogy at his funeral; it is his daily life. To him, Christ's words, "If you continue in my word you shall indeed be my disciples and you shall know the truth and the truth shall make you free," make feigned virtue abhorrent, and flattery a tasteless joke. He is a free man. He is not forced to his actions by public opinion, by a prodding threat from the chancery, by desire for acceptance or the edification of others, or by desire for the enhancement of his reputation. He is compelled by what is truthful and right because of his love for the One who is the way, the truth, and the life.

The same priest does not have to be kneeling before the Blessed Sacrament to be in the presence of God. He has already experienced what Christ promised when He said, "If any man love me, my father will love him, and we will come and take up our abode in him." When Christ said, "Where I am there also will my servant be," He meant it. The real servant knows this because he has all the confidence in his master that the experience of the faithful servant provides. Living always in the presence of the master, he is not tempted to subterfuge because he is aware of the penetrating discernment of the master. The genuine servant has no need of subterfuge because the master is the end and purpose of his life.

Such a priest does not need systems or methods of spirituality. It is not that he does not respect the wisdom handed down through the ages related to the development of the

soul, but Christ Himself being the center of his life, he does
not need traditions or the testimony of history to stir him
to goodness of life or the ways of virtue. Living a Christ-
like life is spirituality. He does not have to do violence to
himself to accept the people who come to him. It just never
dawns on him to reject them. He does not have to sacrifice
his pleasures for the work of God because the work of God
is his pleasure.

Countless priests may say that this is dreamer's talk, that
happiness in God is not that easy. But, they forget that the
truly spiritual man has reached the zenith of human maturity
and development. For him ordinary pleasure is a poor distraction from happiness. His faith lived makes dreams superfluous. He is only taking Christ at His word and, like all those
who do, he has simply found out how very true it is. Who
denies this would deny the truth of Scripture. Christ did
not come to confuse men. Nor did He teach a doctrine
which was beyond the ordinary man's intelligence or acceptance. Man does need faith to accept what Christ taught. But
having that faith, the spirituality of Christ is most reasonable,
its requirements are understandable, and with His grace it
is attainable. To believe less is to fail or deny Christ, which
so many good people seem willing to do in the face of the
divine pressure to go all the way.

It is undoubtedly difficult to translate these beliefs into
daily living but, hard or easy, they are the basis for the true
Christian living of both priest and layman. The sooner they
face this, the sooner they will be ready and qualified to go
forth and conquer the world for Christ. Until they face it,
any presentation they make for Christ will be at the worst
fraudulent and at the best ridiculous. God knows that this,
more than anything else, is what is holding the Church back.
The Council can make all the decrees in the world, but it
cannot legislate right living. It can at best try to set up objective standards of morality which are meaningless and empty

unless men are dedicated to living Christ. The Church just cannot by fiat make men spiritual. It can only present Christ to men and let them find their challenge in Him. That presentation is not made in great encyclicals and fine phrases, but in men and women, its members who look like Christ, sound like Christ, and behave like Christ. If men hold back, insisting on their own standards, nothing, no power, no authority, can make them something they are unwilling to be. Christ's saying "learn of me" is not poetry, a beautiful recitation, the prologue for some epic movie or dramatic presentation, but the clear challenge to the man who would be a priest.

Professional religion, like science, has been practiced almost from the beginning of time. It has been as natural for men to worship as to learn. Religion has been handled by weak men using weak instruments in the unending search for truth, in a constant effort to make meaningful contact with the truth which is God. In the Church, the weak men with the weak instruments have been the moral theologians. And while their casuistry can be condemned as hair-splitting, it has been as necessary to the practice of moral theology as the cadaver has been to medicine. With all the talk about principles and objectivity, existential moral theology and situational ethics, the proper measurements of mortal and venial sin, the dimensions and meaning of sin, the fact and consequence of sin, realism and spiritual fantasy, there is an attempt to discredit moral theology because it appears not to be meeting the challenges of the day. No science does. It is the goal of science to meet the challenges of tomorrow. Scientists are stimulated by the unmet challenges of today to meet those of tomorrow. However, many of the faithful and not a few religious are bothered by the slowness of theologians to react to the stimulus. Some are not reacting because of their satisfaction with the status quo. Others, insecure and afraid to tamper with anything which might draw them away from the safe, hard reality of the teething ring, resist the meat and potatoes of twentieth-century theology. These attitudes are unacceptable for several reasons.

First of all, sin cannot be talked about as objectively as one would talk about apples and oranges. Is there really such a thing as objective sin in the scholastic sense? The moral theologians have tried to take care of this problem by differentiating between material and formal sin. The difference could be well illustrated by the case of a blind man who actually and honestly thought that the woman in bed with him was his wife. The moral theologians would say that his act of sexual intercourse with her was materially sinful but not formally so. Actually there was no sin at all. Sin is essentially a matter of conscience, not just behavior. Sin involves an intentional offense against God. No one sins by honest error. Sin is of its nature malicious. There can be no sin where there is no malice, no deliberate ill-will. Actual sin can never therefore be separated from the subjective as theologians tend to do.

The scholastic distinction between the subjective and objective has been a happy and healthy one, for many reasons and for many years. But now it is only as valid as other distinctions which have proved inadequate with time. Developments in the fields of psychology, human behavior, intention, and motivation, as well as medicine and psychiatry, have opened up vast areas for reconsideration relative to sin. Nothing will permit or justify the closing or reduction of these areas. Was St. Thomas Aquinas' celebrated bulk the grossness of a frustrated, compulsive eater, or was it the result of absent-minded preoccupation with deep thoughts while engaged in eating? Were the flagellations and extreme penances of many of the saints the work of morally good masochists or misguided escapists? While there can be objective standards of behavior, there can never be objective standards of sinfulness. The subjective intentions and motives so inseparable from sin, as well as the knowledge and will required for it, too easily escape the competence of the human judge. Often they are also beyond the understanding even of the sinner himself.

The scholastics would define objective sin as the evil act as it happened; subjective sin as the act which the sinner understood and fully intended, and therefore of which he was guilty. But the evil of an act should never be confused with the injustice of the act, its unfortunateness or tragedy. It must be identified only with its badness; that is, with its deliberate contrariness to God's known and accepted will. The failure to see and accept this distinction has led to the conviction by Catholic authorities that the approval of birth-control devices and contraception is the approval of intrinsic evil, and that, therefore, those advocating these things are perpetrators of intrinsic evil. This attitude has been incomprehensible to those who are equally amazed at the tolerance of St. Thomas and the Latin world toward houses of prostitution in order to minimize the physical and moral consequences of man's incurable sexual concupiscence.

An act is objective, but an actual sin is in the mind and the will of the sinner. Crime is objective but sin is subjective. For example, a murder as a crime is recorded in the police files and reported in the daily press. The murder is a fact but there can be grave doubt about the existence of the sin of murder. One man is dead after another, for some reason, picked up an ax and swung it at his head. The crime is evident but the sin is not. Did this man with full knowledge and malice aforethought coldly calculate the death of the person slain? Or did a crazy man run into the street with an ax in his hand and swing at the first passerby? Or did a fireman accidentally let his ax slip out the window of the building in which he was firefighting? All these things change the nature of the act although the fact of the act, a man killed by an ax, is not changed. For sin there must be a person who does something which he fully realizes is forbidden by God's law. Only two persons are in any way capable of judging the actual fact of the sin, the sinner and God.

The tendency to make sin strictly, or even primarily, objective has had an emotionally crippling effect on many people with a healthy respect both for virtue and for sin. This has been very evident in the matter of "impurity." Since sex and sexual morality have been taught rather badly, and the sexual revolution has put emphasis on how badly, there has been quite an easy tendency to consider sex itself wrong, rather than sin. Sex has therefore tended to seem a bad rather than a good thing. Since adultery, fornication, incest, and bestiality all involve sexual intercourse, not surprisingly the "good" person somehow or other gets the feeling that sexual intercourse, rather than sin, is the problem. Therefore many otherwise very fine people have a puritanical outlook on sex. They are much like the rabid teetotaler who, moved by the anguish of hurtful family experience, considers liquor itself, rather than its abuse, the evil. This is making the thing rather than the person sinful. Yet the sin lies in the abuse of something perfectly good in itself. Fire can be used to cook the dinner or to burn the house down, but neither use can make fire a bad thing.

Things are not evil, but people may be. Acts are not wrong, but sin is. This confusion prompts the quandary between the virtue of killing an enemy in time of war and the sin of killing an enemy in time of peace, the heroism of killing a national enemy and the sinfulness of killing a personal enemy. The act is essentially the same. The same confusion is seen in weighing the rightness or wrongness of capital punishment. The most convinced supporter of capital punishment does not want any part in the actual execution of the convicted criminal, even though he might not hesitate to kill in defense of the innocent. The ultimate decision on capital punishment will not necessarily be right or even acceptable. But it will be permissible because man can only use the best judgment he has, regardless of its fallibility.

Therefore many believe that moral theology, in its honest efforts to teach the principles of religion, has failed to take the subjectivity of sin into proper consideration. This failure has led to the quite erroneous notion of the priest as a judge in confession. The priest does not judge the sinfulness of the penitent; he merely listens to the judgment the sinner has passed on himself. After all, few come to confession who have not already passed judgment on themselves. The priest merely hears the judgment. If the penitent cannot be sure of his sins, surely the priest cannot be sure of them either, for his knowledge of them comes almost completely from the penitent himself.

The tendency to make objective standards of morality govern sin as well as public acts or behavior has led to the confusion between respectability and the state of grace. It has caused pride to become a virtue rather than a vice. It has made getting caught an evil, rather than doing wrong. Sin, which is something personal, private, between the soul and God, has become a matter for shame rather than sorrow. Overemphasis on objective morality has led people to conform rather than to develop convictions. Good men live by convictions; weak men conform in order to survive. The overemphasis on objective morality has shifted the importance from what one is to what one does; it has made piosity more desirable than holiness.

Because there is something obviously wrong about this state of affairs, many are beginning to give it the thought it requires. Intelligent and sincere Catholics, who once accepted the mortal sinfulness of deliberately eating meat on Friday, are now asking whether anyone's eternal damnation should have been equated with such a minor matter as a dietary restriction. This may appear to challenge the whole concept of ecclesiastical authority, but the fact is that the

average person eating meat on Friday had no such thing in
mind. He was merely displaying his unwillingness to deny
himself this small pleasure, or he had developed a degree of
indifference to this specific precept. It was certainly no denial
of God or religious authority. No one aware of Christ's death
for men on the cross could see Him condemning men to hell
for such a minor issue. However legal is one's bent of mind it
is hard to reconcile such a condemnation with charity. One
cannot reasonably insist that the teachings of the moral theologians on this point have been dishonest or uncalled for,
for even with the change in the law it is still possible for a
man to be showing his contempt for the death of Christ on
the cross by eating meat on Friday. But theologians' judgments
have only been as valid as men's judgments can be, and they
are as far from God's judgments as men's judgments must
be. Now these judgments are being rightly questioned, as
in other days they were not.

The Church has made too much effort to legislate virtue
and too little effort to inspire it. This has been notably the
case in the theology of the sacraments. Because the sacraments of their nature give grace, they have become a sign of
grace in the recipients however unworthy they might be. This
is what makes the daily communicant sometimes the most
troublesome person in the parish, and brings holiness into
disrepute. Because of holy orders, the unwary too readily
credit the priest with goodness. As to any other Christian,
goodness comes to the priest through God's grace coupled
with the honest and efficacious effort to practice virtue. Unwittingly and almost imperceptibly, there has crept into the
Church a certain mechanistic sacramentalism. However good
this was in the fight against Jansenism, it has tended to
obliterate Christ's terms for Christian living, the demands
of true holiness.

The Church has seemed more consistently willing to condemn than Christ ever was. For example, Christ's conditions

for the forgiveness of sin are very plain. Sinners are forgiven insofar as they themselves forgive. This does not promise much to the man who would condemn his fellowman to hell for eating meat on Friday. Christ's reply to the woman taken in adultery supports this assertion. "Has no man condemned you? No man, Lord. Neither then will I condemn you. Go in peace and sin no more." Certainly the Scriptures are to be preferred to the moral theologians. And let us face the fact that they have not been. As a result every priest has met countless Christians so frightened of God and His judgment that they can hardly get themselves on an airplane, even though they are fairly good people and certainly not candidates for eternity in hell. Another result is that a moral theologian of repute can be quoted by a magazine as saying that to smoke ten or more cigarettes a day could be mortally sinful because it involves an unnecessary and serious risk to one's health. This, of course, is highly amusing when people know that priests are among the heaviest smokers, and that to live in New York City is equivalent to smoking forty cigarettes a day because of the air pollution!

Something must be done to come up with new and better measurements for sin. Abject apologies should not be required for erroneous teaching by theologians, any more than they were demanded for the erroneous teaching of scientists who once taught that the world was flat. Progress was made when they admitted they could be wrong. They then got to work to discover what shape the world was. The scientists admitted error without surrendering their status or authority. This is what theologians must learn to do. They must courageously and forthrightly admit their mistakes but make sure that moral theology itself is not rejected. It would be a pity if it were rejected because it is as necessary and as valid as ever.

One of the main culprits in leading moral theology to a near impasse is the too widely quoted and accepted qualification of sin as "of its very nature mortal." This is not the place to discover the origin of this qualification, however good and helpful it may have been at one time. Now we know that, regardless of the fact that certain sins can, for teaching purposes, be called mortal by their very nature, it is quite invalid to insist that any man who commits this sin commits mortal sin. All the subjective elements of sin have to be actually present for such a verdict to be correct. And no power on earth can adequately determine all the subjective elements in any sin.

Certain diseases were once considered rightly to be fatal (mortal), and they still are, where the newly discovered treatments and medicines are not available. A sickness in other times was no less fatal because now there is a cure for it. No one questions the conviction men once had that such and such an act was done under "the proper conditions" for mortal sin, but today we have a far different notion of what "the proper conditions" involve. Depth psychology alone has unearthed countless reasons to question the subjective responsibility for things which were commonly considered to have been done with full malice aforethought. Judgment on such actions is therefore more realistic and understanding than heretofore. Again we do not question the authority or the genuineness of the theologians' convictions; we only question their validity.

Sin can be judged by God alone because it involves the consent of the subject for reasons he himself often cannot plumb with certainty.

Nor have theologians yet decided sensibly how much less than complete and free knowledge and consent must be to be truly called "full." Yet who can guess the number of times a confessor, incapable of judging the fullness of knowledge or consent, to say nothing of the other countless imponderables involved in sin, has erroneously forbidden the sacraments to those who need them most in their effort to return to the fullness of charity.

Nowhere is this problem highlighted more plainly than in the teachings of the Church on birth control. There is agitation everywhere for moral certainty in regard to this problem. The Pope and the Council were agitated because of the obvious unrest among the faithful. Confessors are agitated because they are being faced daily with the need for explicit direction and guidance. The people themselves are agitated because of the pressures on them to do something which cannot be delayed or separated from the innumerable and real pressures of daily living. Yet this is a matter which can have no moral certainty other than that given by the authority established by Jesus Christ. If under God, a confessor has the right and duty to give advice that is possibly in honest error, then surely the Holy Father, with the explicit mandate of God, has the power to put the minds of people at ease without the absolute assurance that he is correct in the physical and scientific aspects of the case. It is only in the moral order that the Pope must be right, and he has assurance of that from Jesus Christ Himself.

Some of the people of God are embarrassed that the Church has stood so adamantly against artificial birth control, but there would seem to be little real cause for this embarrassment. Not even the genuine scientist can claim that artificial birth control has been any real answer to the overall problems of man, including overpopulation. Birth control itself has so many imponderable ramifications, personal, public, social, economic, that only an idiot could approve it unconditionally. If, in fact, unrestricted use of contraceptives would lead eventually to unsanctioned indulgence in sex, the consequences of such indulgence could set man back a whole millenium. Like the wonder drugs, which have so detoured man from the short road to the grave that he is in imminent danger of thinking he can live forever in good health, no one knows the ultimate consequences for good or evil of the unrestricted use of contraceptives. But the problem is here and has to be dealt with. The Church has to face the new urgency about it. It has taken a fairly intransigent stand so far, but there can be no question that its mind is open to its new aspects. Despite the charges that it has stood steadfastly and unconditionally against it, the present anguished restudy of the matter indicates otherwise. Its people in millions, both because of it and despite it, are practicing birth control. Now the Church has called for study of the matter in the greatest detail by the most respected and impartial authorities in this world. It is its intention to announce what it honestly and sincerely believes ought to be said about it. However, in the meantime its people have been following its guidelines only with the greatest difficulty and docility. So much has this been the case that the Church leaders, right up to Pope Paul VI himself, have insisted that nothing must be allowed to come in the way of an early and right answer to this most vexatious problem.

Now, if the leading Catholic authorities, at the invitation of the Pope himself, cannot come up with a certain answer, how can one expect the simple, unlettered millions of Catholics living daily with the problem in the intimate relationship of the home and family to come up with something certain? Thus it becomes evident that practicing birth control reluctantly, as people do, under the severe pressure of physical, mental, and emotional health, economy, good marital relations, social and parental responsibilities, they have reason to doubt their guilt of serious sin. In other words, if the best brains and integrity in the Church cannot assure the world that artificial birth control itself is always mortally sinful, and the Pope for this reason alone has to delay an answer which he himself says is of the greatest urgency, what can the simple person, under tremendous immediate pressure and compulsion, do about it? Who can deny that he has a reasonable doubt?

In any case, even the most ardent devotee of birth control

cannot deny the many positive objections to it. No birth control device, in itself, makes love more spontaneous and enjoyable. Many of them represent a physical and psychological separation in an act which is essentially one of union and communion. Man rises to his highest stature bearing the heaviest burden he can carry with reasonable comfort. Contraceptives are an avenue of escape from responsibilities that men need for their best development and finest interpersonal relationships. General indulgence does nothing for a world needing more personal control and responsibility. The issue is clear when the reason for birth control is mere enjoyment. But if it is a preferable alternative to something less desirable, if it is one solution to a distressing problem, a solution more acceptable than its obvious alternatives, then all the teaching of the Church, the urgings of the Pope, bishops, and priests cannot convince the people that it is mortally sinful.

The Church bridles at the suggestion that its teaching authority can be questioned, that it is not necessarily efficacious, that people simply do not have to abide by it unless they are really convinced that they must do so. The practical teaching Church denies that it is possible for people to honestly question it in such matters as birth control. And this when priests themselves admit to no compelling reason to accept in their personal lives the actual restrictions placed on them by the example of Jesus Christ and the evangelical counsels. In 2000 years of teaching Christian virtue, the Church has not been able to make its own teachers and preachers so pure that they do not sin. In the years of enforced celibacy the Church has not succeeded in raising up priests who, to a man, fulfill their obligations in this department. But it does expect the simple, uneducated people somehow or other to understand the evils of birth control, practiced under great distress and difficulty. Such a way of thinking is typically sacerdotal and authoritarian, but it is hardly realistic. Certainly it is not very Christ-like.

The Church's primary anxiety, at the moment, is not for
the salvation of souls. It is primarily a matter of the prestige
of the teaching authority. It seems that it should not be
called into question so easily by so many in such a normal
difficulty as this, a difficulty faced by the way, by no bishop
or priest of the Latin rite, or by the Pope himself. But the
familiar ways of men in power make it plain that the Church
could continue on its stubborn way until few were left to
take her very seriously because its ruling members have taken
themselves too seriously. The Church will be held in the
highest repute when its teacher-leaders obviously hold Jesus
Christ in high enough repute to take His teachings seriously
in their own lives. This has been said time and time again
through the ages by every Christ-loving critic of the Church.
But it is generally written off as an inadmissible argument, as
irrelevant, illogical, or unacceptable. It is very hard indeed
for those who claim authority in the name of Jesus Christ to
impress others if Jesus Christ Himself has not obviously
impressed them. They claim His divinity to support their
power, and their own humanity to explain their weakness.
The Church has never gone into eclipse except through the
blindness of its shepherds. That same blindness is present
today as the Church is consumed with dry rot because the
authorities do not choose to face the obvious facts.

These words are said neither in contempt nor cynicism,
but in wonder at the continued exercise of authority in a way
so certain when it condemns but so unsure when it should
ponder and pardon. No sane man envies the responsibilities
that go with power, but duty is the same for the leader as the
follower. The tragedy occurs when the big burden is laid on
the fragile back, and more so when the wisdom of the fragile
mind is outstripped by its ambition. Perhaps prosperity is
only harmful to the Church. Perhaps, for its preservation, the
Church must reach a nadir from which it begins all over

again. However this may be, the people of God pay a great penalty when authority, for any reason, is more anxious about the people's bonds than about qualifying them for freedom.

To sum up, there simply cannot be mortal sin unless, with serious matter, there is full knowledge and full consent. However serious the matter the Church says may be involved in any question of morality, that seriousness alone can never make a sin mortal. No one can say for sure how complete consent must be to be considered full, or how full knowledge must be to be considered adequate for mortal sin, beyond the fact that fullness in itself would seem to indicate a lack of nothing. Few things that a man does are quite complete or perfect, even his sins, which would have to be so to make hell, eternal damnation, a just and reasonable thing. And hell must be essentially the choice of the sinner, not of God, who gave His Son to redeem men from it. The denial of this has forced many to resort to the denial of the existence of hell, or even worse, to the denial of the existence of such a God as would so punish someone He has professed to love. However meaningful the vaunted visions of the mystics who had seen portrayed, in their intellectual, imaginary, or real visions, countless souls dropping into hell like snowflakes, it remains true that no one goes to hell who does not choose to do so, nor does anyone go there by accident, or end up there without rightly deserving to. Just as no man can enter heaven who is not perfectly good, ready for absorption in God, so no one goes to hell who has the slightest degree of the love of God in him, who is not, in a word, perfectly evil. It takes but the slightest love of God to make man perfectible, and this slightest love is not easily lost. This is, and has been, the teaching of the Church. But it has been neglected in the well-meaning efforts of many righteous moral teachers presuming to interpret the mind of God for the people of God. Somehow or other their interpretation always falls short of the picture of the Father portrayed by the Christ who at His Father's insistence died on the cross for love of men.

The moral theologians have to make judgments worthy of Jesus Christ whose religion they teach. The legal, casuistic approach is more talmudic than evangelical. The law of love is to dominate in Christianity rather than legal technicality, to which most people so easily respond with fear. The stimulus of fear, however, cannot be maintained long without man's developing an immunity against it, and the loveless religion which inspires it must sooner or later be discarded.

The moral theology of the parish is that which reconciles sinners to God, gives them hope, inspires them with the real worth of the good life, and brings its own special rewards. The Christian pattern for happiness promises happiness in the here and now as well as in eternity. Serious sin is not something done primarily by ignorant, indifferent people but by able, malicious people. The former we have in almost unlimited abundance. The latter, however numerous, are still rare enough to be considered more sick than sinful, even though sickness makes them no less difficult to handle. Moral theologians are no more expected to be infallible than loving parents can be expected to know the right mixture of kindness and severity demanded in the raising of a retarded child. Those not claiming infallibility should be more reconciled to fallibility than most moralists have been. When God, by giving man his personal freedom, made him responsible for his eternal destiny, He did not wait until man was as mature as he is in the twentieth century, nor did He supply to each his personal theologian. He provided him with a conscience and a judgment to be perfected by trial and error, retaining to Himself the ultimate judgment on every man's success or failure in coping with the challenge.

The moral theologians may have inadvertently concluded, or at least considered, that their way was better, but when they seem more severe than God there is little wonder that

people are so inclined to bypass them and depend on God
for judgment. The Church, the parish, and the priests should
be there to offer all God's gifts to those who wish to be better
people, holding back from none the help they need to
succeed in this one important thing.

Chapter 7

Canon Law

IT IS fervently hoped that legalism in the Church reached its peak with the promulgation of the New Code of Canon Law in 1918. Uniformity of law in the Church brought great relief from unnecessary confusion. However, as must always be the case, flaws are soon exposed in the best laws of men which are powerless to eliminate human weaknesses. Frequently the law produces side effects which make the wisdom of the original law seem doubtful. Prohibition gave birth to bootlegging, gangsterism, and the Mafia in America. It is generally recognized today that when the law becomes more restrictive of freedom than protective of it, every man has lost something which is a part of his very nature, God's own gift. Certainly the dire straits to which the teaching of blind obedience in religious life has brought the state of religion should be evidence enough that no one can interfere with liberty without damaging man in an essential area.

The problem of avoiding excessive legalism is a difficult one wherever good order is required, and there is no dispensation from the problem. So today there is much evidence of the sincere effort to avoid not only damaging restrictions but ineffectual and superfluous ones. The detailed, prescribed routine in seminaries is being dropped as unsuited to the preparation of priests for the modern apostolate. There is general pressure from all sides to eliminate penal laws related to many fundamental obligations such as public worship and penitential practices. It is said by those urging the repeal of penalties invoked, or allowing the laws to fall into disuse, that the fulfillment of basic Christian obligations should come from increased love of God and the desire to accomplish the duties of one's state. It is insisted that the invoking of penalties and sanctions alienates rather than influences people. The arguments pro and con are many and thought-provoking.

The impossibility of legislating virtue has been acknowledged. The efficacy of invoking fear in relation to things of the spirit is doubted. The power of love has admittedly never been seriously tried. Many are concluding that if the Christian religion cannot become strong and produce happy people through the inspiration of love it is doomed to wane and fail. It would appear necessary now to give it a fair trial in circumstances about as ideal as can be hoped for. But the possibility of the falling away of large numbers of the so-called faithful, the monetary loss, and the lessening of the political influence of the Church make many responsible and thoughtful leaders hesitant in a matter in which they have little choice. State religions all receive the ignominy heaped on governments; they are failures everywhere that democracy is at work. And democracy is at work everywhere. People in power have used religion to serve their purposes from the beginning of time. Subjects have either feared it enough to give it lip service and the required minimums, or loved it enough to make it a real part of their lives despite governmental influence.

Goodness, like truth, cannot contradict itself. What is for the real good of the individual cannot be to the detriment of the Church or the people of God. The Church does not need, and cannot afford, to practice the very thing she condemns in tyrannical totalitarianism. The Church is for the good of the individual. Therefore the law should favor the individual; his good should be paramount. The law which gives any priest the faculties to hear a person's confession in danger of death should give any priest the faculties to hear a confession which is for the real good of the penitent, the spiritual welfare of the sinner. The Church should be more eager for the greater good of all than merely to eliminate abuses, however necessary it may be to do that. The abuses coming from such a law would be minimal and there are many ways of handling them. It should be left to the judgment of the confessor to decide what is and is not a true need.

It is said that the sacraments must be safeguarded. The individual soul should be cared for before the sacrament. After all, the sacraments are for the people. Christ Himself did not call on the twelve legions of angels to save Him from abuse. No minister of the sacraments is going to abuse them unless he himself is indifferent to their use. In that case, it is the minister rather than the suppliant soul who should be penalized. The sacraments are holy things but they do not need the safeguarding that souls require. Christ spent Himself and his grace lavishly on the people. His Church should do the same thing. Freely it has received, freely it should give.

The legislation dealing with marriage is primarily directed toward the safeguarding of the sacrament, and only secondarily toward the good of the individuals involved. The all-too-familiar result of this is the actual inability of the poor and ignorant to seek legal redress in marriage cases. The Church has been roundly abused for favoring the rich in handling marriage cases. Every priest of integrity resents this abuse. Reality clearly shows that it is the rich who are able to understand and undertake the long and tedious processes of law relating to the marriage bond. The rich are usually educated, understand the processes, and can obtain the services of qualified people to handle their affairs. So the law does favor the rich, intentionally or not. What harm would be done if through error some decision in a special case favored the people rather than the sacrament?

No reasonable person questions that the poor can get the legal help necessary to solve their problems; the poor simply do not seek redress because of ignorance or inertia. The legal process is beyond the comprehension of many of the poor, who live daily with troubles of every sort which dispose them to accept frustration and leave them with little expectation of assistance. They seldom reach the stage of attacking the problem intellectually because they have lived primarily on the emotional level. In fact, when one tries to determine at what stage a person is able and willing to settle for present due processes of ecclesiastical marriage law, he quickly realizes that few people make use of them at any stage. In the face of the difficulties involved, most people simply conclude that it is not worth the effort and settle for civil processes, or no processes at all.

In all cases of real doubt, the doubt should favor the people. The sacrament must be safeguarded, all other things being equal, but not at the cost of the people. After all, God spared nothing for the people, not even His divine Son. Many people make bad confessions in the sense that they are dishonest, incomplete, with omissions through fear or pride. But the priest feels no onus to determine, with certainty, that every confession is honest and complete. He believes the penitent. Otherwise the sacrament becomes odious. Few confessions are bad through malice, for the man who knowingly and willingly makes a bad confession only does harm to himself. Most bad confessions are made through ignorance or weakness. So the man who makes a bad marriage, or escapes a valid one dishonestly, does himself harm. The problem is his, not the Church's. And apart from modest safeguards for the sacrament, the law should not be written to make it impossible for the good person, in an unfortunate and invalid marriage, to have it set aside because some legal technicality is missing. If the appointed judges decide honestly that there is, in all probability, no valid marriage, it should be set aside. There is no question that the primary difficulty here is the jealousy of the Church for its good name as the upholder of justice and the law. But the law the Church should uphold is the law of love, which works for the best interests of the individual soul.

A celibate clergy must face the fact that man has virtually irrepressible sexual desires and needs, and that God has made him that way. Only a man of great virtue (and how many of these exist even among the clergy?), a most unusual man, can live chastely outside of marriage. This being the case, when there is real doubt the marriage laws must favor the people rather than the marriage. If men antagonistic to the Church want to call its use of annulment "Catholic divorce," what does it matter? Only the pride of the self-righteous demands that the world see that the laws are administered without respect of person and with all legal propriety. But Christ's whole ministry was primarily personal and not legalistic. He frequently expressed contempt for the legalism of the Pharisees and rebuked their disrespect for charity. To resist the legalistic approach to the law's administration is not to recommend that the laws be weakened to the point of emptiness, or administered capriciously. It is only to recommend that the law give every consideration to the people rather than be canonized as an absolute measurement in itself.

Just as many people do not have the knowledge and will-power to commit a mortal sin, so many do not have sufficient understanding to enter a Christian marriage validly. This truth is much more apparent in our time than it was in the past. While the Church can never openly or legally approve trial or companionate marriage, or whatever name is used for such a pact, the Church does in practice allow many mar riages which took place out of proper form to break up as the surely must and do. On appeal, the prior civil or religious ceremony out of proper form is declared null and void. The Church fervently hopes that the second marriage, this time under proper form and auspices, will be more successful and happier. Who is going to say that doing so is wrong? However, if a marriage can be easily and quickly annulled on the technicality of form, when in reality the parties had a witnessed marriage in which they gave consent without reserve or condition, nullity could also be declared when it could be reasonably shown that a marriage under proper form took place between two people who did not have sufficient knowledge of what they were doing to assume the lifetime bond of Christian marriage.

If a nun makes a final vow in religion, a public formal declaration that she irrevocably gives her life to God, she can still be dispensed for reasonable causes and without undue delay. Surely a young girl, married without a fraction of the preparation or understanding of the nun, could have her marriage rightly annulled for lack of sufficient knowledge for full and proper consent. Nor should the sacredness of marriage itself prevent this, for surely the fullness of knowledge and consent are essential to its sacredness and inviolability. No Protestant or pagan child could be said to profane the Blessed Sacrament because he receives the sacred host not understanding what he is really doing.

Those who categorize the use of annulment by the Church as Catholic divorce do so with some truth. Catholics jealous of the good name of the Church resent this, but the difference is only technical; in fact, they are virtually the same. It is a legal device put to good use. But if, because of the weight of public opinion, the Church now recognizes the validity of marriages under almost any conditions, a great disservice will be rendered Christian marriage. There will be countless victims of legal marriages which are marriages in name only. It is not that marriages before civil authorities or other Christian ministers should not be recognized as valid; it is just that it is far more important to make the validity of a Christian marriage depend on the knowledge and intention of the parties. It should not be impossible for subsequent circumstances to bring proof to light that one party to the marriage, or both, kept hidden things which would have made the actual consent invalid. If the Church now faces the fact that priests must be dispensed from their vows and allowed, for most reasonable causes, to be married despite their well-intended vow of celibacy, it can do no less for married people whose marriages could be correctly judged invalid for causes which are equally reasonable and right. Christ gave the Church the power to exercise mercy in the ministry of love. It should not hesitate to use its power in behalf of sinners wishing to love and serve God. And if it would appear that many, appealing to its use of this power, were fakers and phonies, that is another matter and problem. People can be amply warned that such dishonest appeal to power profits them nothing. Their sin, after all, is something between themselves and the God who can neither deceive nor be deceived.

For many and weighty reasons more realistic legislation will be forthcoming. This will not be done to encourage low regard for the married state, the marriage bond, or the institution. It will be to make it possible to determine with greater accuracy the real impediments to true Christian marriage, to make it possible to judge where a true bond exists and where it does not.

In Church and civil law it is possible to unite in marriage children of fifteen years or even less. Even when he is completely convinced that such marriages have little or no chance of success the priest is bound to perform the marriage. Many of these children marry because of premarital pregnancy or compelling emotional causes which make free consent next to impossible, yet once these people are married by the priest and the marriage is consummated there is no appeal from it. Such marriages should generally not be permitted, even if both parties are determined to be united in a civil ceremony. If the marriage turns out well and the parties wish to renew their vows properly at some later date when they are more mature and understand what they are doing, it could be so arranged. Surely at least the same conditions required for mortal sin, which is, of its nature, a responsible act, should be required for the unbreakable commitment of one's years here on earth to another person. No one incapable of mortal sin is capable of such an irreversible commitment. The law should say so. That such legislation is difficult does not dispense from the duty to enact it.

In a very honest effort to meet the problem of proper and responsible consent, the chanceries of the world have produced many premarital questionnaires. Nothing so points up the legal mind and the mistakes of lawmakers as these questionnaires. In the first place, the finest questionnaire cannot obviate the difficulty of shortcomings in the candidates for marriage. Furthermore, the questionnaires are loaded in favor of the law, making the answer "yes" inevitable even when it is meaningless. These questionnaires are presented for the sake of the administration rather than for the good of the people involved. Their length and detail reveal the chancery mentality and language and technicality beyond the average member of the Church. In mission lands especially, the questionaires are ridiculous. The priest himself might fill them out neatly for the record, but certainly not the simple people of primitive cultures, many of whom are incapable even of signing their names. Surely no amount of legislation will replace the instruction of the people in preparation for such a serious obligation as is marriage. Nor can people whose life is in no sense Christian, and whose fidelity to Christian worship is negligible, have much appreciation of Christian marriage, its fact or its obligations. Moralists can appreciate the impossibility of making converts from paganism sufficiently aware of the seriousness of the obligation to worship publicly with weekly regularity. And so they rightly state that those who cannot comprehend such an obligation are not seriously bound to it. Yet this same principle is not applicable in the areas of old established Christianity where proper instruction and example are assumed even where they are nonexistent or ineffective.

The mind of the celibate reveals itself in the handling of marriage cases before Church courts. These cases are treated as if time were not an element at all in the lives of the people. Surely there is sufficient knowledge of regular court procedure, and enough competence, to resolve these cases in minimal time with minimal investigation. The fact that such service is not easily available drives people to civil divorces and, despite good faith and the desire to remain, drives them from the Church. The religious, social, moral, and psychological penalties to the children are quite heavy.

Einstein is reported to have said that nothing is discovered until an axiom is questioned. Law is the canonization of tradition which precludes the questioning of axioms or of anything with an aura of age or wisdom surrounding it. Yet law governs the living of modern man. Laws are seldom abrogated or repealed; they remain on the books and merely fall into disuse. This does not matter so much in civil law. But in this day, when time is so precious, the great danger is that, when a few laws of the Church are disrespected because of their uselessness, the whole of Church law may fall quickly into disuse or disregard.

The laws governing clerics and religious are a good example of this. Surely, if nothing else, the cleric should be a man of his times and of the place he works. Such things as his garb and his general approach to the apostolate should never be legislated from Rome. Fanaticism about the wearing of religious garb has far outstripped the clergy's earnestness about the spiritual life. Yet until very recent days, the cleric dressing like a real man has been merely tolerated. Vatican II has been somewhat realistic about making regional conferences of bishops responsible for these trivial decisions as well as many others. But it took the assembly of world bishops to force this through, and even then it was not the principle of garb which was a stake, but the fear in Rome that total authority was slipping from the hands of the Curia. Requiring appeal to Rome in matters in which the competence is not in Rome but in the area in which the matter originates is what would seem to make this new recognition more breeched than observed. As clerics have not been trained or encouraged to be original thinkers, neither have the bishops been trained or encouraged to use their prerogatives and powers of decision in the application of law to local conditions. The local Church suffers greatly as a consequence.

The whole law relating to clerics and religious has emphasized, beyond all proportion, the obligations of subjects and the powers and rights of superiors. Subjects have been aware of and willing to fulfill their obligations, even though they have been generally oppressed, encouraged not to think, to limit their vision to the immediate future and the immediate chore, to avoid exploratory thought and productive curiosity, to leave the investment of their talents entirely to their superiors, and to make only minimal private or personal judgments. Superiors have found themselves accorded high diplomatic immunity and approval in principle for whatever they might do or think, and the right to command without consultation. The law must acknowledge that this is a new age with different standards which are neither negative nor anarchical. The law must catch up with these. It is the era of cooperators, shared profits and benefits, the pooling of the talents of all for the greater good. All these things must be under the direction of authority, but the right of investigation and appeal must be assured at all levels. To delay suitable legislation for this era is to make the mistake of the capitalists two genera-

tions ago. It is to refuse arbitration and rapprochement
between the two sides until such arbitration is forced on
authority in circumstances quite unacceptable to it. Capital
forced labor to seek the power it now has, and that certainly
is not an unmixed blessing. If economic inflation comes to
the world today, it will be because labor has proved in its turn
as intransigent as capital. It will be due to the repetition by
labor of the unnecessary errors of primitive capitalists enjoy-
ing the "divine right of kings" to stand above all question,
doubt, or investigation.

The laws governing general chapters, elections, and secrecy
all must be changed to assure better government for the
religious orders of the Church. The chapters of religious
orders are so set up that the community is represented by
delegates and ex officio members with an average age of 60
years and more. How can these people possibly debate and
legislate for people in their twenties and thirties? Representation should be in proportion to the age groups, and from
the age groups. And there should be many other considerations in legislation for more effective organization and management of the groups with such potential for good in the
apostolate.

Canon law must set up reasonable, available, and effective
structures of appeal for subjects. Suffering in the name of
Jesus Christ is part and parcel of spiritual growth and development, but the arbitrary inflicting of that suffering by those
who claim to serve and love Jesus Christ is an abomination.
No Christian should have injustice thrust on him, in the name
of God, by his superiors. But this has been done, without
possibility of appeal, with judgment being passed by the
associates of superiors without adequate investigation, without hearing or weighing evidence or trying other reasonable means of arriving at a verdict. When any subject knows
that he can appeal the arbitrary orders or decisions of a
superior, obedience of the highest order will be possible. The

establishment of these structures will eliminate 70 percent of the whimsy of authority and 50 percent of the rebelliousness of subjects. They could be very easily set up. Far from reducing the prestige and effectiveness of authority, they will increase and enhance it. They will enable those in authority to avoid the unnecessary mistakes which only discredit them. They will provide ample scope for the best use of the talents of subjects and insure their continued use in the best interests of the Church. They would remove the abuse of the human rights of dedicated people which has contributed to the shortage of vocations to the priesthood and religious life.

In establishing these structures, every region of sufficient size to warrant it should have judges appointed to study the appeals. These judges would have jurisdiction directly from the Holy Father and be independent of the local bishops in ex officio conduct of their work. They would never be permitted to hear a case from their own native diocese or religious order. The judges would be competent priests, religious, or lay people as required by the nature of the appeal. Competent women judges would be available in the cases better handled by them, or in which they would have greater competence. Every member of the Church would have access to these courts as the particular situation demanded. The hearings would always be as public and objective as truth, honor, and the best interests of the Church demanded.

In the event the appeal were sustained, the appellant would have clear support from the court, and complete vindication from any charges of rebellion or disobedience. Especially in the case of appeals of priests against their bishops, and religious against their superiors, provision would be made by the court for acceptance into another diocese or religious province, if such became necessary for the good of the persons involved.

Were such courts of appeal approved and established, few bishops would be tempted to abuse their authority. Zeal for the good names of their communities rather than ruthless suppression of complainers and complaints would make religious eager to settle injustices fairly and expeditiously out of court. For no superior, knowing how erroneous or unjust his judgment was, would willingly expose his folly or vindictiveness to public knowledge. Such courts would give a tremendous incentive to charity where it is needed most, in the priesthood and religious life. Such courts would give the seeds of charity time and help to grow into the strong supports for truth and integrity which religious life requires if it is to survive and flourish in the modern world.

The idea here is to point out some possible improvements in a few limited areas while not forgetting that similar things must be done soon in the whole field of Church law. Despite its necessary legalism, the law of the Church must better represent the mind and will of Jesus Christ. Whatever else may be thought or said about the matter, and however difficult legal problems may be, nothing in canon law can replace the law of love which is the one and only law of the New Testament. The very idea of contracts between religious orders and the bishops in whose dioceses they work is repulsive. Such contracts are open admission that charity is not enough to compel even religious to the decisions best representing truth and justice. Perhaps it is time to say that whatever cannot be settled in charity, in the name of God, were best left to wither and die, as it surely must. Certainly the bishop who does not want religious in his diocese can soon be rid of them, and the religious who do not wish to work in a diocese can soon be delivered. The penalty of their absence will be far more effective than any other sanction. The measure of what could and should be done in canon law is only the measure of the goodwill required for the presence of Jesus Christ in the soul.

Chapter 8

The Liturgy

ALTHOUGH the liturgists have been phrenetically insistent for years that the vernacular must be introduced, they have never quite succeeded in putting the word *liturgy* into English or giving it any real meaning for the people. Maybe the Greeks did say it better, but for practical intents and purposes let us settle for the word liturgy meaning the public worship of the Church. The vernacularists were, by far, the most organized and articulate promoters in the Church. Drawn up in battle array, they were just about to begin the fight for something they did not believe they were going to get, when the opposition capitulated. Since the liturgists were better organized for war than for peace, they ended in confusion. Of course, in ending this way they only found themselves, for the first time in years, in harmony with the rest of the Church. It too was in confusion. The liturgists knew everything that was wrong with the liturgy as it had existed, but they had not prepared a new one.

It seems that the public worship of the Church has been considered from a rather narrow, and not too Christian, point of view. The worship of the Church was built up into some-

thing very impressive, despite the fact that God hardly needed
to be impressed. And even if He did, it surely was not man
who would do it. And so the people ended up in somewhat
the same condition as the Jews in relation to the temple of
Solomon. The temple bearing Solomon's name was built to
honor the God who was supposed to be the heart and center
of Jewish life. Nothing of beauty or magnificence was left
out. All who saw it would be duly impressed with the greatness of the God in whose honor such a building was erected.
It was to be the greatest tribute that Solomon could pay to
the God of the Jews. It was to express appreciation for all
that God had done for them. However, as time went on and
the beauty of the temple was the talk of the adjacent
world, the tone of the tribute changed. The people pointed
out the temple as the wonder *they* had created to their God.
Instead of reminding the world of what God had done for
His people, it stood as evidence of all that His people had
done for God. It was, in that light, a pretty silly thing.
Similarly, the worship of the Church has often become something paying tribute to men rather than to God.

Regardless of the magnificence of the Church, the richness
and beauty of the vestments, the lavishness of the altar and its
decorations, and the glory of the music, the Mass can never
be any more than what Christ did very simply at the table in
the Cenacle. He took bread and wine and changed them
into His body and blood to be the food and drink of mankind. No more, no less. The Mass simply cannot have more
meaning than it had then and there. And, of course, the Mass
is nearly meaningless as a form of worship if it does not
establish the reign of God in the heart of man. If man were to
present all his gifts to God in worship and withhold his heart,
he would not so much honor God as dishonor Him. This
seems to be largely forgotten in the liturgy of the Church,
because it is largely forgotten in the lives of the liturgists, the
priests, the bishops, and the people too. The power of the

Church seems to come through much clearer in worship than the power of God. Any religious disintegration which has ever taken place happened only after people honored God with their mouths, while their hearts remained far from Him. In other words, without charity the people of God are nothing. Christ had to remind the Jews that, if being a child of Abraham was their claim to fame, God if He so chose could of the very stones raise up children to Abraham.

So now we have seen a radical and very wonderful change in the public worship of the Church. At long last, the Pope and the bishops have decreed that the Mass and other forms of worship must have more meaning for the people, more reality, more significance in their lives. And they could, too, if the heart of man was more impressive than his mouth. Somewhere in zeal for the vernacular, it has been tragically overlooked that the teachings of Christ were not intended to change the language but the heart. The liturgy will be a great success if the new language and the new rubrics work an iota of change in the hearts of men, more than the old forms did. Whether much good will be accomplished remains to be seen. Nothing can dispense the shepherds of the Church from trying, through worship, to improve men's attitudes and working relations with God. They have tried and are trying. But very much remains to be done.

On considering the liturgical changes, it would appear that several things have been left out. The first and foremost is the development of communications. Never before have so many people been blessed with the availability of music. It is a common sight in the jungles of Africa to see the natives walking to market with their produce on their heads, topped with a transistor radio. No one can question the tremendous possibilities of this development. Communications can be such a power for good. The glad tidings of the gospel can be presented to every nation and in every tongue by the finest intellects in the most understandable language, from every part of the world. Each people can hear the wonderful things of God in his own language accompanied by his own music.

The insatiable appetite of radio and television has consumed the most bountiful output of the greatest talent. In other words, boredom has come through radio and television as it has never come before. It can easily come to public worship too. And it will come, with alarming speed. In no time at all the people will be bored by the new liturgy, bored with the ceremony, bored with the singing and music, bored with the presentation of the doctrine, unless there is a great resurgence of religion itself. Unless there is a very active planning program, the pews could be empty before the Church undertakes what must be done. Intelligent people cannot have the same thing drummed into them day after day like television commercials without turning away for relief. That boredom will come faster with worship in the vernacular than it would with Latin, which represented something accepted over the years, intelligible, but always just beyond the threshhold of understanding.

To see what could happen, let us take as an example the beautiful Christmas carols which have lasted for so many generations. No one ever seemed to tire of them. But with the advent of electronic reproduction systems and high fidelity records a change has taken place. They are everywhere. A few years ago a Jewish radio performer mentioned quite casually, and sincerely, that if he heard "Silent Night" sung one more time he would go out of his mind. He was severely taken to task for his indiscretion and it was insinuated that he was anti-Christian, biased, and bigoted. Yet, every department store, every shopping plaza, and even many public transit systems have these carols blaring forth for nearly two months before Christmas. No one is going to credit the department stores with wanting to encourage the devotion to Christ which is the purpose of the carols. Through commercial use these classic carols have become tedious even to the most devout person with a taste for the beautiful. Religion must not be allowed to become a crashing bore for the people, but must be made a vital factor in their lives. And this cannot be done without budgeting talent, personnel, and money to assure it. Commercial interests have taken over holy things to help their business. The Church should take over commercial things to assure the success of its work. While commercial interests have produced and developed radio and television, the Church has sat on its hands and watched. Typically, it has been quicker to accuse commercial interests of abusing this medium of communication than to use it for its own evangelical work. It has been content to see artistry and talent of all kinds recruited and exploited for commercial ends rather than developed and put to work in the best interests of religion.

People are not too impressed with spectacles any more. They have seen too many through the roving eye of television. Just as a man can stay at home and, from the comfort of an easy chair, see a football game in more detail than by attendance at the game, so too the people have been brought into close-up relationships with the greatest spectacles in the world without leaving home. It will not be too long before the people of the world will have seen everything there is to see. This must be remembered by the authorities in relation to worship and everything surrounding it. There can be nothing secret, nothing hidden, nothing magic any more. Religion will have to stand or fall on the people's awareness of their need for it, and what it alone can do for them. The churches could become garages and parking lots if, through oversight, they lose the power to draw men to God.

Therefore, public worship must change, and be free to change, in every way possible. No longer should decrees forbid anything but a monolithic presentation of some one form of worship, considered worthy of the Church. Somehow or other there must be found a formula to bring public

worship from the heart. There must be found some way
to send a man away from public worship more united to God,
more efficacious in the Christianity of his daily living. The
great and powerful Church in America must change its ways
from fund raising to "good" raising. This will demand a
radical change, but a change which is indispensable, if the
Church is to survive as a real influence in the life of the
nation.

With few exceptions the lives of modern Christians are
just not very impressive. Neither are the lives of priests or
bishops. However important their persons may be, their
Christ-likeness is not too striking. Yet when religion does its
work, this cannot be said; it will not be true. Public worship
will not be made up of empty words but will be the public
manifestation of a truly Christian heart.

It is senseless to say that tremendous progress has been
made by the clergy since the times when popes, bishops, and
priests rode off to war to preserve their material possessions
and prerogatives of office. The fact that countless innocent
and not so innocent ones were slain in those days in the
name of God does not make the clergy look any better today
to people whose only knowledge of history is what they see
with their eyes or read in the history book of the daily press.
Admittedly the secular press is not out to impress the world
with the Christ-like characters of churchmen, but that is no
reason to dedicate a Catholic press to a glorious, if false,
image of the clergy. Churchmen, in the face of the challenge of discontented young religious and lay people, cannot
be satisfied just to remind them by letter from the chancery
to be docile, to be patient. Patience was never the virtue of
the young. The goodness of the clergy must be evident in
other ways besides those contained in their own press releases. The public worship of the Sunday must be an expression of the history of the week, that which was done by the
worshipers in their love of God. The people want to see, or

at least have reason to hope, that the teaching of Jesus Christ can and does have some effect on the men in authority, who then would have something impressive to say about a God in whom they obviously believe. There is not much evident faith in Jesus Christ in those who impose an inflexible set of regulations on a liturgical development, leaving little latitude for the spirit of God in the people.

The Church today should allow its liturgy to be varied, especially in this time of transition when no one really knows what the future demands or history will reveal. We know that what impresses one person in religion can depress or oppress another. Why can there not be, not only church buildings of ultimate simplicity, but forms of worship of ultimate simplicity, which would appeal to the Quaker or Plymouth Brethren type? There is certainly room for real variety. The essential is the Mass which in its original form was a very simple matter indeed. Its meaningfulness and profundity were once as impressive as its simplicity. While lavishness of ceremony honoring God may have its place, so may the simplicity which much better represents a God in whom simplicity is personified. To say that a proliferation of ceremonies and ritual will make the Church all but unrecognizable may be true, but it may also be false. No one has yet panicked because the behavior of many Christians has made a mockery of Christianity.

A reasonable way to start might be with a very simple ritual with minimal decorative symbolism, such as was used by chaplains in time of war or under persecution. It could also extend to a very lavish presentation, dignified and conveying some of the tremendous depth of meaning in the Mass. Nor would there be anything wrong with a nice quiet, old-fashioned, peaceful Mass in Latin for the people happy in the old way or too set in their ways to change. After all, no one said that the Mass had to be in the vernacular; only that it could be.

A real hangover from the monolithic and somewhat paranoidal days of Catholicism is the necessity for conformity in minor detail lest in some way the essentials be lost. When a decree comes out permitting additional parts of the Mass to be said in the vernacular, every parish must begin on such and such a day regardless of the fact that many may be prepared before that date, while others might only be suitably prepared many weeks later. What is the meaning of the date? It merely lets the world know who is in charge. The importance given this seems to indicate a real insecurity on the part of authority, rather than a reasonable step in implementing the decisions of the Council.

Already we have witnessed the admitted absurdity of chopping up the Mass into bits and pieces of English and Latin in a nearly meaningless way. We are now witnessing the retention of Latin for the priest when in less than a generation few priests will know any Latin at all. We witness a recent move to insist that priests and diocesan seminarians retain the Latin Mass when they are going to work in an area where Mass will always be in the vernacular. Many bishops have sensibly ignored this decree which conveys nothing of the spirit of the Council, and which really indicates reversed vision or nostalgia for the uncontested past. Tranquillity must not be confused with *rigor mortis*. One iota of realism should indicate to all, as it does to me, a confessed former upholder of the Latin Mass, that the vernacular is here to stay. I honestly could not conceive how a change of language would make a difference in the Christian heart, but the Council spoke and there was no choice of motion but forward with the Church. Can any retention of Latin be realistically defended?

One thing which should be done without delay is the presentation of Sacred Scripture in a more complete way through the daily Mass. While proper translations and books are being prepared, the widest latitude should be allowed in the matter of translations and even the quantity of Scripture to be used, with virtual freedom of choice in the matter of scriptural selections at the parish level. What difference would it make if this were permitted for a period of several years while experts were working on a better presentation of everything? It would certainly give the experts something to study, and it would make the parish a practical laboratory productive of many wonderful things.

Special scriptural selections could be made for those Masses which are fully attended on Sundays, holy days of obligations, and other special occasions. Briefer and more pointed selections could be made perhaps *ad libitum* for private Masses, much like the former choice of additional orations in votive Masses. Masses for small places with meager attendance could have Scripture readings in keeping with the instructions to be given or the religious education needed. The prayers of the Masses, in which there are many disjointed selections from Sacred Scripture mostly taken from the Psalms and the Old Testament, and in which there is little meaning or dignity, should be rounded out and made meaningful. There should be nothing empty, disjointed, or uninspiring in the Mass.

There has been a tendency to canonize meaningless tradition in the worship of the Church. This is an argument for dropping only the meaningless, not for casting out tradition. But religious worship should be prophetic as well as commemorative. The hopes for the future should be spoken of as well as the events of the past. The whole uncertain future of man must be put before him as a challenge to his fidelity. The scientific symbolism of the modern world should be blessed and incorporated into the worship of God. History has little appeal for the youth of the world which considers as historic the happenings of a mere twenty years ago. Just as all of us have been bored to death by the often repeated tales of the senile or near senile, so youth has little patience with continued harping on the past when it knows perfectly well that the best and most important part of its living is in the future. Recorded history loses its real significance when disconnected from the present and the future.

America could hardly be more conscious than it is of the tax load. And in view of the Great Society, where it would seem that even the laziest person in the country is not to be permitted to do without anything he wants, many people are frustrated by the increasingly large penalty paid by the energetic, talented, and productive person. The merits and demerits of such a system can be argued back and forth forever on every kind of principle without arriving at any economic or social conclusions which time and experience might not prove wrong. However, of one thing we can be sure, taxation has detached a lot of people from their money. It has developed in them the mentality, "We might as well spend it and enjoy ourselves because the government is going to get it anyway." It has also been the occasion, if not the cause, of tremendous private fortunes being channeled into charities and foundations of many sorts. It has awakened people to the necessity of paying for the good life. Surely it should not be hard to make the average, responsible citizen nearly as aware of his tax debt to God in his obligation to worship publicly. Yet more and more thinking people are concerned about private worship in the lives of the people of God.

Perhaps private devotion and personal sanctity are seen with a jaundiced eye because of the widespread discrepancy between the lives of so-called holy and devout people and the teachings of Jesus Christ relating to charity and the love of neighbor. But the paraliturgical ceremonies and personal devotions which take up the slack from public worship are not so much a side issue as no issue at all these days. This is distressing to many who realize that, while we attend public buffets and state dinners, we also have to eat regularly at home. Religion is not so much a matter of public worship as it is a matter of daily living. The teaching of Christ did not so much insist upon fitting liturgical ceremonies as it did on the primacy of love of God and neighbor. These can be the outcome of long and faithful public worship if that worship is carried into all aspects of the day-to-day living of the Christian.

The Christian was told that he should pray without ceasing, which could only mean that his life was to be his prayer. His life was to be one of union with God, of worship, of private worship. In one's zeal for the public worship of God, one cannot for a moment think that private worship does not matter. This would be akin to saying that as long as a husband and a wife present a loving public image, it really does not matter how they get along together privately, whether they really love each other or not. Their public life, if it is not hypocrisy, is only the public manifestation of their private life. In his private worship a man's Christianity really shows, from moment to moment, day to day, from one human act blessed by Christ's teaching to another.

The paraliturgical devotions are to be encouraged although not necessarily increased or multiplied. Here again there has to be room for individual taste and temperament. History may produce, but it must never canonize, the inane or superstitious. Only error is to be avoided. There must still be a place in the Church for new devotions as there was in the day of St. Francis of Assisi for the Christmas crib and the Way of the Cross. When someone as great as St. Francis comes along, and we must never believe that God will not bring forth others just as great, there will be these new devotions.

However distasteful to me personally is the cursillo, it unquestionably offers something highly estimable and productive. Surely as the Great Society flourishes and poverty is outlawed and hunger is a thing of the past, the corporal works of mercy must extend to the emotionally poor, hungry, and underprivileged. Although money will be put into the pockets of the now poor, depriving them of one of the greatest stimuli to progress, there will continue unabated, if not increased, the real poverty of the masses in their need for love. The apostolate to the withdrawn will replace the apostolate to the shut-in, now largely fulfilled by the companionship of radio and television. The kindness and consideration for the needy next-door neighbor will be replaced by the concern for the very different but very needy man next door in Africa or Asia. The jet plane has made getting to him easier and more urgent; it has mocked distance and established unavoidable communication; it has made his presence and his needs inescapable to the would-be isolationist. The apostolate will not be so much to the far reaches of the earth as to the far reaches of the mind. The spiritual actor, artist, and writer will become the missionary.

Industry was once considered, without much justification, the monstrous dragon devouring the downtrodden laborer and enriching the squires of the mechanized world. Things have changed now, and labor has not only rights but powers as awesome as those of the squires. Management has had to find a formula for survival, and the formula has been "diversification." The liturgy presents the Church with the opportunity for diversification and perhaps survival. This diversification, well directed, will not only turn up many new avenues of progress for the Church, but it will help it praise God as nature does, in its diversity. And, if the world is truly God's, its worship of Him must not be the closely defined performance of a single man or a single group of men. It must be the worship set out by the Son and assured by the continued presence of the Spirit sanctifying and guiding the redeemed people of God. It must come, too, from the hearts of men, but in a manner and in a setting they can understand and love.

This then will be the liturgy, in all its glory, giving to men what, of its nature, and under its limitations, it can give, but never seeming to do what it simply cannot do. For the liturgy is but the form of worship. Worship itself must come from the heart.

Chapter 9

Catholic Education

NOTE. There is a great difference between Catholic education in Canada and the United States. The big difference is in the financing of the schools. Generally in Canada there are public schools and separate public schools. The latter are, of course, the Catholic schools, except in Catholic areas where the public schools are Catholic and the Protestant or nondenominational schools are separate public schools. These schools are all supported by the government up to the tenth grade or so; the education taxes of the minorities are used, as democratically they should be, for the schools of their choice with the government making the appropriate grants required to maintain proper standards. In the United States, however, all Catholic schools are considered private schools and are generally supported entirely by the funds collected through tuition, parish contributions, or diocesan assessments. There is the penalty for the Catholic in the United States, therefore, of having to support the public school system as well as the Catholic school system. There are other differences from place to place which need not be considered here, since they do not have much bearing on what is discussed.

The very term *Catholic education* is material for disagreement. The quarrel could be the typical quibble of the hypercritical, who avoids clarity and purpose because he needs the shelter of confusion for his argument, but there is something to be said for the inacceptability of the term. Few will question that education, to be education, must be catholic. That is to say that the field of education must be as broad as the work, experience, and progress of man, and therefore catholic in the literal sense of the word. Therefore, no education can be true education if it omits the field of religion. For, like it or not, religion is as much a part of human life as is sex, nutrition, academic training, or any other essential of life. Whoever doubts or questions this exposes his ignorance of the history of man. Certainly, religion cannot be dismissed by some intellectual crackpot who, in a day when any wise man knows his own limitations, has the effrontery to think he knows everything, or worse, can be so naïve and ridiculous as to solemnly proclaim that "God is dead." Through education, men must seek the truth, and, for the man who honestly does so, it is fairly difficult to come to much truth without approaching the Truth, who is God. But it would appear that Catholic education would more rightly be called *education of Catholics.*

It is the failure to make a distinction that has caused education to be so oriented religiously or politically that it is second-rate. It is as difficult and emotionally costly to avoid bias and prejudice in education as it is difficult and costly to isolate a virus. The atheistic educator can no more keep his hate of God and religion out of education than the Catholic educator can keep his love of God and his own prejudices out of Catholic education. Education can be so oriented toward religion that it presents errors in the guise of truth to cover the embarrassment or wishful thinking of fanatics. When it does this it is hardly worthy of the name of education. Those responsible have never understood that the truth needs no defense, does not fear exposure, while error has no defense. Again, like it or not, justifiably or not, Catholic education for the very highest motives, but often with dubious erudition, objectivity, and pedagogy, has presented a subjective brand of education in many fields. Certainly it has not shown much eagerness to reveal the venality and perfidy of many of its historic leaders.

Because of many understandable and even praiseworthy factors, the Church has used education primarily as a means of getting the message of Christ to the people to whom it has been sent. Naturally, then, education in the Church has been heavily tilted toward the priesthood and the apostolate. But most of the people educated by the Church were not only not going to be priests; most of them were not going to be apostolic laymen. Another purpose of Catholic education was to make it possible for Catholics to take their places creditably in the life of society around them. This was not possible in the early days of America when education was not available to the poor immigrants. The Church was, therefore, compelled to provide this education, and did so at tremendous cost in people and money to itself and to the apostolate. Today it is still very difficult in America for the really poor to get a Catholic education, but they do have access to the public schools.

Now that public education is everywhere available, there is much to be said for the Catholic people's making use of it. There is relatively little anti-Catholic prejudice in it because of the position and prestige of the Church in America. It also has the funds for relatively higher academic standards than are everywhere available in Catholic education. There should also be good Catholic teachers in these places. Not only would they be impressive witnesses to the beliefs which shaped their lives, but they would represent the Church in a way and place in which it has not had much representation or recognition. If more of her members went to these institutions of learning as pupils and teachers, the Church would have to be more alert to provide their religious instruction, either through special arrangements with the educational authorities or in some other way. If the time of the Sunday sermon became more vital in religion, our people might hear some interesting and informative sermons instead of the poor fare they are now suffering so often and in so many places.

Certainly the segregation of children in Catholic schools to save their faith is not an unqualified success. One of the immediate results is that generally the less fervent and impressive Catholics go to public schools and this does not lead to a very high esteem of the Church. If the Catholic teacher in the public schools is also a third-rate Catholic instead of the very best, the same thing will apply. Catholic children tend to have less respect for their faith when they are segregated in Catholic schools, than they do when they find it challenged by those around them. That is why the best Catholics in the world seem to come from the predominantly Protestant areas such as Northern Ireland, Protestant Holland, and Catholic enclaves in the Far East. It is not that Catholic schools cannot or do not produce good Catholics. It is just that doing so is not inevitable. Those beliefs which everyone has and holds seem to be valued less through familiarity and lack of challenge, as is the case with Catholicism in Catholic schools.

Apart from all this, it can hardly be estimated how the schools have impoverished the Church. Their cost is astronomical. The money involved could accomplish tremendous things in the mission fields, to say nothing of what it could do at home through the use of radio and television, and other apostolic projects. But the greater impoverishment has come in the expenditure of human resources and talent, not measurable in monetary terms. Many of our ablest people are wasted in the business of providing and administering just the buildings used and money spent in the cause of education, while the children of the kingdom asking for bread are being given stones. And the staggering thing is that this has been done till recently without question, without deep and thorough examination of the value of such a system. Rome can well look with envy on the vigor of the Church in America and the lavish support of the Church by the people, but to credit the parochial school system almost alone for this is a mistake. There are a great many other factors contributing to the vigor of the faith and the support of the Church, starting right back with the faith of the immigrants and the spirit of people eager and determined to succeed, to raise their standard of living through education and hard work.

If the parochial school system is to be blessed and made holy it should not be through error in judgment. It should not lead people to expect something of it which it is powerless to produce, or to depend on it almost exclusively for the progress of the Church. Although it is true that the money consumed by this system would not necessarily be given to the Church for its work in other fields, still any productive project in the apostolate would find ample support. America is known for its desire to win, its desire to cooperate in a going concern, its love for the prestige of success. There are many other apostolic projects to be tried. But few of them will be tried as long as Catholic education takes such a big bite out of the funds and personnel of the Church in America.

At whatever meetings and in whatever circumstances someone has the temerity to question the basic value of the schools in the overall picture of American Catholicism, he finds himself accused of irreverence for the sacred cow of Catholic education. Until now Catholic education has not been studied in depth for its inherent worth. It took the Carnegie Foundation to make the grant leading to the recently published

Greeley-Rossi report, *The Education of Catholic Americans,* and the Notre Dame study, *Catholic Schools in Action.* This study should have been undertaken long ago as pure common sense by the Church itself. No commercial enterprise investing a small percentage of the billions poured into Catholic education would have done so without a long and earnest look at the project.

The Greeley-Rossi report has been "received with great interest," according to the Catholic press, but it will be generally unread even by the people concerned, like so many encyclicals and conciliar documents. The report wisely states that the idea of Catholic schools is so deeply entrenched in the American Catholic mind that they will continue regardless of criticism. Little will be done, despite the fact that the preface to the report indicates that it does not "come down firmly either for or against the Catholic school system."

To question the accepted policy of Catholic education in America has been equated with heresy. It has been equated with questioning the authority of the bishops and the Church. Yet we have seen the policy in Catholic education proven wrong time after time, only to be smugly blessed with praise for the rapidity with which it has adjusted to reality. Its error could hardly have been more evident than it has been in the matter of sex education. When this course was first given impetus by the godless government of Communist-dominated Mexico, it was excoriated as the basest immorality and as seduction of the innocent. Yet we have to admit that in the failure to provide adequate (whatever that means) education in the field of sex for our children, we denied them access to the facts they needed to prepare them for an essential part of living. No one has publicly admitted how wrong we have been. The senseless sexual revolution is now in full swing primarily because of this denial of such important knowledge to the children. And we are now building homes and shelters for the unwed mothers who might have been able to avoid these places had they had the knowledge they needed. Of course we insisted that sex education was primarily the responsibility of the parents who were even less equipped to teach their children than the priests and nuns. The parents themselves knew little enough about the facts, except what they had learned from personal experience, which was considered either too personal or too shameful to talk about to children.

When someone makes a study in depth of the purpose and efficacy of Catholic schools, and proves that they are fulfilling that purpose with reasonably high effectiveness, then they will be worth the price in personnel, material, and money poured into them. Support for them will be unequivocal. Under the old type of authority no one would be permitted to suggest such a study, let alone inaugurate it and hope to be assisted. The current situation of Catholic education arose from decisions made in different times and circumstances, and those decisions involving the sacredness of tradition could not be questioned. But if they remain unquestioned, the Church in America might pass beyond the point of no return. Even if it should be proven that the parochial school is the best and wisest investment of people, money, and time, still research, examination, and experiment on a broad scale should continue, for surely there are better ways and means of making the Christian message effective in the world than have been undertaken thus far.

At one time the possibility of having educated Catholic men as a force in the world was negligible without this big investment in education. Now, a hundred years later, we have available thousands of educated Catholic men who are totally wasted in the program of the Church because it would appear that they are not needed enough to be used by the clergy. This attitude on the part of the clergy has led to the lack of priests (if there is such a lack), because so little use has been made of the laity. Surely a Church wealthy enough to operate a school system like that of the Catholic Church is rich enough to employ highly qualified Catholic laymen in the program. And they would be employed, except for the notion that the Church belongs to the clergy which must have full administrative control of the school system. In other words, the Church is the responsibility of the clergy, and it is still considered so, at a time when we know that, by definition, the Church is the people of God.

Now the challenge of education is clearly before the Church. It will have to make up its mind whether it is going down with a system it has blessed, or whether it will move with the times and advance. The production of leaders is the phase which must replace the education of the masses as a prime concern. There must be a temporary exception for the education of the colored masses. They require another twenty years of the unstinting dedication of religious that white Catholics have enjoyed for a hundred years. If the nuns would modernize their habits which frighten and repel and make them an anachronism in the world, and then go into the colored areas as qualified teachers, in whatever educational facilities would be provided, public or private, they could develop a harvest of responsible colored Catholics. This work could make up for the general and almost unbelievable neglect of the Negro by the Church for the last two hundred years. This assistance would be deeply appreciated by all those who are dedicated to the academic development of the Negro in the United States. If this dedication cannot be found among the nuns, it is nowhere in the Church. There is a notable shortage of nuns, even for the present Catholic school system, but if the work for and with the Negroes is done generously, a by-product of it might well be the renewal of religious life in America. The fact that people willing to do this job well would have to be real people (which many of our nuns are not) could purify the lives of our religious Catholic educators.

There is the tremendous problem of costs for Catholic education. This is draining the Church of its financial resources. But, as has been said, the real drain is on its resources of personnel. Its best talent is being wasted in public service instead of being used in the apostolate. For the education of American Catholics *is* a public service. The idea that public money cannot be used for parochial schools is ridiculous. The money is public because it comes from the public and is to be used for the public. What a mockery of democracy it is when a few dissidents can insist that no public money is to be used for the promotion of religion, as if religion were not worthy of the protection that pornography gets. Freedom of religion does not mean freedom from religion. Education demands the teaching of mathematics; it should also demand the teaching of religion in the sense that no one can possibly understand the world he lives in if he does not understand the meaning and place of religion in that world.

There should be a federation of religious schools which would operate as a public system for those millions of Americans who want their children educated with the humanizing influence of religion. To say that such a thing could not be done is to say that parents do not have the right to indicate the manner of the education of their own children. Such a system works in Canada and other countries; it could work well in the United States. Any government does wisely to avoid a monolithic public system of education. The very idea of monopolies is so un-American that the merger of industrial giants is considered by the government to be against the best interests of the people. Surely, to remove competition in the field of education is to deprive it of one of the fundamental stimuli to greatness and superiority. There should be at least two or three systems of public schools all providing the basic requirements of education but leaving the way open for competition and better development. The cost of a privately supported system of education is too high a price to pay for both the Church and the country.

The public school system needs the influence of religious men and women in its work for the best interests of the country. The Catholic Church will never have its proper influence unless its people are studying and teaching on state campuses and in secular universities and colleges. The argument that this is already happening is not quite valid. The extent to which it is happening is the extent to which it has been made inevitable by the inability of the Catholic institutions to expand sufficiently to accommodate Catholics wanting a higher education under their auspices, and the necessity of such high tuition fees to maintain those less than adequate faculties and facilities. Large segments of the people of God are sending their children to the public schools because of this. Also, it is generally a fact that neither the poor nor the less intellectually endowed can find Catholic schooling. This situation will worsen as the cost of education increases and the Catholic schools are forced to continue with little or no assistance from public funds.

Lay teachers working in Catholic schools pay a penalty, but not only on the level of wages, pensions, and fringe benefits. Their leader potential is simply not developed because they are working in a clerically dominated system where their qualities of leadership are seldom wanted. The lay teacher well used in the Catholic school or college is the exception rather than the rule. Unfortunately, too, many of the Catholic teachers now in public schools are antagonistic to the Catholic system, and anticlerical besides. There are those also who are Catholic in name only. Thus both Catholic schools and public schools are deprived of the best Catholic teachers.

The bishops are far from unanimous on the question of state aid for the schools, even though the schools cannot

long survive without it. It should be made very clear that
the bishops and Catholics are seeking aid for education, not
for religious education. Also it must be laymen who do the
negotiating with the government officials, and this cannot be
done until and unless the Catholic schools are directed by
school boards almost entirely made up of laymen who are
both zealous and capable. Religion is highly esteemed by a
tremendous segment of the American public, and the idea
of producing intelligent and articulate Christian leaders regardless of denomination, will become increasingly appealing
to thoughtful Christians as the present trend to eliminate
religion entirely from the public school system continues.
The religious schools will appeal as the great leaven needed
in the educational system of the country. As religion rather
than denominationalism becomes more important, the public
will be more amenable to the idea of supporting schools
which have, along with acceptable academic qualifications,
religion as an important part of their curricula. Although
religious schools should have no greater claim to public aid
than have the present public schools, they should not be
penalized because they are religious schools any more than
a bonus should be paid to the godless ones.

It appears that, even now, many bishops do not realize that
persecution of the Church in America is a thing of the past.
Only mild paranoia can permit anyone in authority to believe that the Church is persecuted, can prevent one from
seeing that people are more afraid of the Church and its
power than against it. Because the Church does not receive
the state aid necessary for excellence in its schools, the
Catholic authorities feel discriminated against or persecuted
when those schools are called second-rate or worse. When
the bishops realize that they need state aid to produce excellence, perhaps they will be able to persuade the government
that it cannot afford to deny to any school the opportunity
to produce it. American society can absorb any amount of

excellence coming from Catholic colleges, but that excellence has to be produced in something besides football and basketball before Catholic education will be very impressive. The bishops must make up their minds whether they can produce excellent Catholics in their own institutions, which are at best second-rate, or whether they must at last deliberately send Catholic students into the highly-endowed secular universities to achieve academic excellence in competition with their fellow Americans. In the past there has been the tendency to "hot-house" Catholics in order to save their faith without realizing that faith which has to be "hot-housed" has little chance of survival in a materialistic world. Opposition to it in secular schools is the challenge it needs to make it strong. While being protective of the faith of our Catholics by insisting on Catholic education, we have certainly failed to carry the message of Christ into the secular universities where it really needs to be heard.

In other words, Catholics have been trying too hard to save themselves and therefore, not surprisingly, have to a great extent lost themselves as Christ said they would. Just as Christ, being lifted up, was to draw all things to Himself, just as Christ died that we might live, so Catholics must go into the secular colleges and accept challenges to their faith so that Christ might be a factor in those seats of learning from which He is virtually excluded only by default. As far as religion is concerned, the secular colleges have long been like the child of neglectful parents; when he needs them, they do not help him; and when he does not need them, they are there to join him. When, despite their neglect, he becomes successful, they then want to take credit for his success and share it with him. He resents this, and so is religion resented in the secular establishments of learning. The very best Catholics should be encouraged both to teach on the state campuses and to attend their colleges. Catholic colleges, if there must be Catholic colleges, should be for those whose religious life has been previously neglected or undiscovered.

A strange thing in Catholic schools is that religion itself has often been the subject most poorly taught. Since religion is the primary purpose of the Catholic school, there is ample reason for putting the most skilled and inspiring teachers in charge of religious education. Neglect of this has brought us to the present situation where the bright Catholic students are bored silly by religion, and the schools themselves have failed to turn out the large numbers of informed Catholic laity needed in an intensely religious work. Many can trace apostasy to the bad impression of religion they received in Catholic schools.

One of the basic causes for the poor quality of teaching in Catholic schools is that too few of the religious are truly teachers. Because so many schools are operated by religious, those who enter religion are made to teach even though they are not so inclined or qualified. No religious should be a teacher unless he or she wishes to be, and is qualified to be. The inbred education of Catholic colleges is not enough to equip a teacher for the work. He or she must be qualified by the best courses available. Teachers have a native weakness by vocation. They tend to be communicators rather than thinkers. They communicate only what they have learned. And this weakness, coupled with their exaggerated classroom prestige as oracles, tends to make pygmies look like giants. Education in the secular universities would help to reduce religious teachers to their actual, proper size.

Unfortunately, in an attempt to match the excellence of the secular universities the Catholic schools have begun accepting only the brightest boys and girls. These are sought out in much the same way as athletes are or were recruited not so long ago. And the students with the best financial standing are more welcome than the poor. It is well known everywhere that the brightest students are often not the best balanced, nor are the financially well off always the most personally sound. Consequently, too much of the investment of Catholic education has been directed to those who will benefit by it least. The secular universities have already accepted this fact and are working sedulously to remedy the situation. They are offering scholarships to the needy and opportunity for the educable, knowing that many of the country's potential problems can be turned into assets by such a program, with enormous savings to the citizens. They also know there is a wealth of talent to be tapped if the opportunity for education is available to all. Surely religion should provide enough humility for Catholic educators to be the first to see their mistakes and the most eager to remedy them. But this is almost impossible if the policy of Catholic education is made by authorities who are not educators and who are not generally in sympathy with the real problems involved.

The magisterium of the American Church must come up with some long-range plan for Catholicity in American education, which is what their plan should be called instead of the plan for American Catholic education. But as long as the captive Catholic press must insist on the automatic excellence of everything Catholic regardless of objective standards and truth, those in authority will never realize what a bad job they are doing. And they are doing a bad job, not because they are incapable of doing a good one, but simply because they are the last to get the message. The proximity of the layman to, and the welcome he gets from, those in authority is in direct proportion to his willing capacity for flattery and adulation. For anyone who could doubt this I am sure that a look at the empty honors lavished by the authorities on their faithful flatterers makes the truth too obvious to question. Has anyone heard of the faithful priest, critical of his bishop, being made a monsignor before he is too old to care any more? Has anyone heard of the layman, vocally demanding a better job of those in authority, being

made a Knight Commander of St. Gregory? It goes without
saying that the answer is in the negative. Certainly no one
can expect a sane man to reward his enemies, but are a man's
critics necessarily his enemies? They have generally been considered so by churchmen. And the penalty to the Church for
this has been tremendous. Industry is delighted when a critic
proves his charges because it enables industry to correct its
costly mistakes and assures success. But few critics of the
Church are given the opportunity to make, much less prove,
their charges. Such charges should be welcome if they involve
improvement in the administration or conduct of the Church.
Nowhere has the Church paid a higher price for this attitude
than in education.

There is undoubtedly a place for Catholic education as it
is now known. Whether there should be an all-out effort to
provide the United States and Canada with four or five
regional universities of the highest standards, instead of
proliferating small colleges of dubious value, is an important
question still awaiting an answer. Whether or not Catholic
colleges should be on, or close to, state campuses and an
affiliation worked out whereby existing facilities are used by
Catholic students registered through their own colleges at
these places is another valid question. Whether Catholic
colleges should join the privately endowed colleges of high
repute and follow the above plan is yet another question to
be answered. And there are many more questions which,
when answered forthrightly, will set up the shape of things
to come and make cohesive planning possible. Such answers
must be honestly sought and made known. And when they
are, many people will come forth who are willing to work
toward the desired goal. Then mature religious will be found
to dedicate their lives to such causes as education which
represents the best possible education for Catholics.

Chapter 10

The Church and Money

IF THERE was ever a story of rags to riches and riches to rags, it has been that of the Catholic Church. The graph of its rise and fall financially would look like the ocean waves. It is like the Jewish nation of Old Testament times; when its people were faithful to God it prospered, and when it prospered its problem was to live with prosperity. When Christ said that it was harder for a rich man to get into heaven than for a camel to pass through the eye of a needle, He was preaching detachment. He did not condemn the rich; He just said that being rich made it harder to be good. God knows that the Church in its early days lived off the wealth of Joseph of Arimathea and other benefactors. It was not itself rich. Today it is rich. The recent publicity given the financial status of the Vatican at 5.6 billion American dollars shook up a lot of people. It shook them up even more when it was made known that this sum did not include any of the priceless items in the Vatican museum and art treasury. Naturally many Americans, sensitive about the part America has played in shoring up the Vatican's finances, were as wrong as they were quick to claim that that was where the American money was going. Apart from the fact that American churchmen are willing to surrender only a very small percentage of their money to any outside beneficiary, it turned out that this impressive figure represented only the money which Mussolini had paid the Vatican as indemnity for the papal states. It had been carefully husbanded through shrewd investment to the fantastic figure mentioned above. Without the skillful handling that it got and the mercy that history showed it, it could have ended up worthless or evaporated after World War II, but this made little difference to the critic. The fact remains that it is a rich Church and riches always present problems.

The Church is therefore in the position that it is damned if it does and equally damned if it does not. When a deeply spiritual bishop refuses to concern himself with the finances of the diocese and leaves behind him a financial mess, the people complain about the bad handling of the finances. When a successor is appointed to take care of the mess, and does so with intelligence and astuteness, people are quick to talk about the wealth of the Church. They remark that it is really big business. Of course it is. But that does not stop it from also being real religion. It just means that the Church faces the problem of every person who is financially successful. It has to manage its own success virtuously; it has to come to a working agreement with money which is the very stuff of living in the modern world. The day of the offertory gifts and barter is over and done, and regardless of the effort to understand the symbolism of the ceremony of presenting the firstfruits of the land, money is here to stay as the material of gifts. The Christian principle of giving has not changed, so the Church will always have money. But neither has the Christian principle changed of being the master, not the slave, of money. So the Church must use its money well, not investing it in power but consuming it in service. The theology of handling money is not one thing for the individual and another thing for the Church. Yet there persists some remarkably old-fashioned thinking about this.

The Church is very slow to face the requirements of public trust, operating everywhere but in tyrannical or totalitarian governments. Those standing in the place of God, considering themselves accountable to God alone, have overlooked their accountability to the people of God for the use of the funds placed in their care for the work of the Church. Obedience is a sacred obligation of the Christian, but irresponsible wielding of authority has brought the very obligation into doubt. Contributing to the support of the Church and its works is a very sacred and indispensable obligation of the Christian, but the irresponsible handling of contributed funds, made possible by the refusal of the Church to publish financial statements, has not only caused the world some scandal but has made the obligation to give more honored in the breach than the observance. There have been near disastrous consequences of this refusal, both spiritual and material. Not only have people gradually ceased supporting the Church, allowing vast areas of the world to go hungry for the word of God, as well as bread, but governments have undertaken the support of the Church in many countries. The government, where it supports the Church, finds it easy to subvert it to its own ends. Thus religion has gone hand in hand with colonialism. This has brought down on religion the hate of the colonized for the oppressor power. It has also tended to encourage, in the missionary, some contempt for the conquered people. Imperialism, once respected as power, has used the docility taught by the Church as an opium for the national aspirations of conquered nations. Empires have paid for this mistake. So has the Church.

The Church has left herself open to many accusations supported by more than a little truth. Whenever and wherever her star has risen with that of imperialism, it is hardly surprising that it has also come perilously close to setting with that star. When the Church has depended on the financial blessing of secular governments for its missionary endeavors, there can

be little wonder that its policies have been identified with
them. Given the doubtful protection of the then godless
government of France during the Boxer Rebellion, the
Church became identified with that godless government.
Much to the joy of the needy French missionary bishops,
the Church received large sums of indemnity money through
the treaty levies against the Chinese. Not surprisingly, those
bishops found themselves, along with France, the butt of the
hatred of a people who saw little Christianity in the cry for
indemnity by a Church which professed to teach people to
turn the other cheek to injustice. Surely France cannot by
any means be singled out as the only country to have brought
grief to the Church. History books are filled with such incidents and episodes. The picture of the Holy Father himself
blessing the flags and armies before the Italian invasion of
Ethiopia still strikes the most devoted sons of the Church
with mystification and some shame.

The point being made is that the Church has the deeply
fundamental obligation to subsidize and operate her own
programs of charity. When the Church in America undertakes a school system which impoverishes itself, it also renders
itself incapable of undertaking programs in the missions,
which should be her responsibility from start to finish. However praiseworthy the work of the Peace Corps, and however
hard the American government works to keep the Corps
separate from the State Department or other functions of
government, it will always be identified with the American
government and its interests as long as the finances for it
come from that government. Although it is the desire of the
American government to have other governments participate
or have their own similiar programs, it can not convince the
aided people of its altruism while it is the first and most influential power in the programs of assistance. Despite its
position as the most prestigious power in the world, and the
wealthiest nation, half success or less is all it can expect in

aiding less fortunate people. The only other organization capable, at the moment, of assembling the personnel and facilities for a worldwide program is the Catholic Church. Yet such a thing is impossible until the Church comes to grips with its own financial problems.

Christ stated unequivocally that if a man would be perfect he was to go sell what he had and give to the poor and come follow Him, yet the 'question of the Christian and wealth has been puzzled and pondered over without anyone coming up with a clear-cut answer. Perhaps a clear-cut individual answer is impossible because the obligations to perfection of each Christian are his own. However, there can be no question as to the necessity of some degree of detachment from material things. In other words, when these become an obstacle to salvation, rather than an aid to it, they are to be cut away and disposed of. Christ did not say that material things could not be an aid to salvation. Greed is not the sin of the rich alone. The poor can be far greedier than the rich; they can certainly be more covetous. There has been far too great a tendency to condemn the rich because of the envy their riches inspire rather than because of the evils associated with those riches. Just as the condemnation of sexual sin has tended to sound more like the condemnation of sex than sin, so also the condemnation of avarice has tended to sound too much like the condemnation of riches. Sex is good, and so are riches. Both are the handiwork of God. Through the former, man is challenged to purity and the growth of true love. Through the latter, he is challenged to detachment and the best use of wealth for the good of all. When Christian poverty has been preached by the Church so steadfastly, it is all the more a scandal for the people to see the Church and its administrators living the high life, which, regardless of all the explanations in the world, only money can buy. It is amazing how many gyrations in logic sensitive churchmen can go through before they admit the obvious, that they do in many instances have the good life, and that they like it and intend to keep it that way. The failure to read the signs of the times has been the great factor in the repeated eclipse of the Church, her periodic return to rags.

Just as the individual Christian has to face the tough decision about riches in his own life and his attitude toward money, so does the Church have to face the decision about the proportion between the income and the output, between the value of investment in things of this world and investment in the things of the next. Those responsible for the best investment of the Church's money to secure the funds required for its proper operation have to make this decision. Nothing will permit them to delay or forget it. Nor can they delegate it to others. Nor is it so much harder a decision to make than the personal one. However, unless the people involved have made their personal decisions, there is little likelihood of their making the corporate one; this, of course, to the serious detriment of the work of the Church.

There is so much symbolism in religion that there is a general tendency to accept the symbolic, the legal, or the ideal for the real. This is especially true in the lives of professional religious. Taking the vow of poverty can so easily be equated with living the virtue of poverty, yet there is a world of difference between the two. The failure to think realistically has led, in religion, to the anachronism of priests dispensing themselves from the virtue of poverty which they are solemnly bound to practice not by vow or legal obligation, but by reason of their professing Christianity before the world.

The desire for ownership or private property is natural to man. So is his basic desire for this world's goods. But these desires cannot be wisely handled without a very specific confrontation with Christian principles. Therefore, like it or not, the day that a church, bishop, or pastor does not wish to make a public financial statement, this confrontation is

being avoided. There is reason for the one in charge to fear
that his work will not stand scrutiny. The scrutiny of the
inescapable eye of God, to which everything is open and
naked, is the highly commendable expectation of the Christian. Many people are rightly grateful that they will be judged
by God rather than their neighbor, who often finds mercy
beyond his capacity. Still, God's judgment will always be
easier for the one willing to face the judgment of his people
on his fiscal administration. Certainly those who pass over
this opportunity are forgoing one of the greatest safeguards
of the soul, a real stimulus to the practice of virtue and the
cultivation of integrity in particular. The demands of the
public can be extremely exasperating, but they can also be
the best insurance against one's own great weaknesses.

The world has continually witnessed shocking corruption
in public office almost everywhere. Therefore there is an in-
clination to believe that the world is going from bad to worse.
But this only seems so because there are more people whose
acts are more public. The ubiquitous and unappeasable eye
of television is exposing material which in other days simply
would not have been brought to light. The law enforcement
agencies are working more effectively and protectively than
ever. Escape from the consequences of wrongdoing is more
difficult. The exposure of the wrongdoing of many highly
placed people is causing young people to be disenchanted
with their elders. They are unwilling to listen to people
living the double standard. This is to be regretted, for wisdom
is no less wisdom because it comes from a person somewhat
less than a saint. The demands of the news media for scandal
for their readers and their listeners and the exposing of what
was once considered one's private business are forcing people
to meet ever higher standards of public conduct. These same
revealing means do force many who are unwilling to raise
their standards to ever greater ingenuity in hiding from public
scrutiny, but it ill behooves churchmen to be among those

having to hide from scrutiny. Avoiding it is a luxury the Church can ill afford. The detailed press coverage given Vatican II regrettably made front page news of the dissension and strife among the Fathers, but it quite happily made progress inevitable just because of the awareness of those Fathers that very little could be hidden from view.

The properties of money have also changed. At one time usury was considered against nature because money could not breed and multiply as animals did. Therefore its natural increment was considered nil. Today we know that money does breed in its own fashion and begets money in such a productive way that natural breeding could never match it. Money can be quickly and effectively applied to innumerable areas of development and production. The Church, like every other organization, cannot afford the luxury of storing its wealth in vaults but must have it working in the world of investments. But it should not bury it so deeply that what is required cannot be instantly available for Christ working in the world. If world economists and merchants understand the value of money in the development of their interests, so also the Church must understand the value of money in the development of its apostolic work. Investments have a way of requiring more investment and the apostle can become the miser when his viewpoint changes and prudence seems to outrank charity for the moment.

The American way of life has gone a long way in raising the standard of human living. The avidity of people everywhere for the good things of life is ample testimony of the esteem of the world. Few of America's bitterest critics willingly dispense with the comforts of its way of life. Most of them churn out their very criticism with an efficiency largely invented or inspired by America. Many of those most critical of America's love of comfort, view their own domains, without objection, from the soft-cushioned seats of air-conditioned Cadillacs. Americans, so willing to pay for luxury, are even more willing to pay for service. Because of this, churchmen must realize that their people require a service quite distinct from mechanical devices. The people are never happy to see an air-conditioned rectory alongside an insufferably hot church, but the thing that makes them even unhappier is the need for air-conditioning the minds of churchmen living in the comforts of the past. America is anxious to share its esteem for advanced mathematics and science with advanced theology and church administration.

Ingenuity in the use of money for the work of religion has not been very noticeable in the Church, but certain priests have met the challenges of the times and, with great thought and hard work, developed a highly organized and deeply personalized parish. Few other priests, however, have made it a point to study their efforts, and to duplicate or improve on them in their own parishes. They are too content with the status quo, happy to wait for another letter from the chancery which they can ignore with a sacerdotal grunt. There are many reasons for this attitude. One of the main reasons is the tight rein on parish finances which has been exercised by the chanceries. The chanceries have steadfastly refused to let others have a say, and sometimes even a thought, about the proper development or handling of the funds required for the excellent job of which many of the priests are capable. Incredible as it seems, there are many dioceses in which the use of funds by the parish priest without the specific OK of the chancery is limited to as little as two hundred dollars. While most pastors ignore this regulation and are doing what must be done in an adult and mature way, still others keep double books and are in a general way handling things just as reprehensibly as is the chancery. In doing this they have been guided by good teachers, but with tragic results. They handle the parish finances as if they were their own private business. The chance of being reprimanded is negligible, depending only on some unfortunate backfire from an ill-chosen, major expenditure, or the revelation of the facts by an untimely death — and in this latter instance, the reprimand is charitably omitted from the eulogy. Chanceries are merciless usually in only two financial situations: scandal from embezzlement, and refusal to meet the quotas set for chancery programs. If the clergy were encouraged by example and instruction in the proper attitude toward money and the joy of the challenge to use it for the glory of God and the good of the people of God, ecclesiastical America would produce the most highly developed religious technology in the world. It would also produce very happy priests and people.

Many bishops have felt an insufferable burden in the financial responsibility for their dioceses. Their penchant for accepting this debt as their personal burden is only equalled by their mistake in assuming complete administrative responsibility for their dioceses. But the administrative burden is no more theirs personally than is the debt. This attitude can be disastrous. It unnecessarily places a very real burden on a man ill-equipped for it, for generally there are men available to the bishops who are well-equipped for this work.

The personal attitude of bishops toward these responsibilities has made them unduly anxious to get out and stay out of debt, and unduly fearful of undertaking good works outside their dioceses. No business enterprise or homeowner can afford this attitude. It minimizes understanding of their problems and the means of meeting them.

Through mistaken judgment incredible sums have been poured into church buildings in America. A generation of clergy, children of poor immigrant parents, can still take great pleasure in these impressive buildings. The fact remains that such buildings still represent a brick and mortar Catholicism, as brittle as the material of which they are built. It is high time to finance the work of the Church beyond the brick and mortar stage, to develop Christianity in depth. Yet it would appear that the planners have a tiger by the tail. Buildings demand more buildings. Perhaps because material building is more tangible than spiritual or moral building, this phase of operations will continue until someone has the courage to make the reassessment for which the situation calls. The steady preoccupation with the fiscal side of administration and the pouring of money into the quicksands of property and buildings have deprived the Church of the research so badly needed in relation to its real work, which is the development of the Christian spirit in the people. This research cannot much longer be deferred without the Church's finding herself with many buildings on her hands but without staff or means to utilize them. Meanwhile, the areas of spiritual development which represent the future and effectiveness of the Church are left unexplored.

The world has seen luxury for the working man on a scale never before dreamed of. This is especially true in America, where the Communists would like to believe that the downtrodden masses are starving. The appetite for the good things available to men has spread to the working class everywhere. In America forty-two percent of outboard motors belong to the working class. Visitors from abroad stare bug-eyed around institutional parking lots at the luxurious cars disgorging crews of maintenance departments. This is a wonderful advance. But the constant fulfillment of material desires leads simply to an insatiable appetite for more material comforts. To avoid this, the spirit of Christian poverty must be esteemed, and the virtue of poverty practiced. And nowhere can Christian poverty be practiced more than in the handling of the purse. Not only must people learn the happiness and joy that can come from sharing, but they must be warned of the awful danger of the disease of discontent with everything that comes from emotional indulgence. The emotions are never satisfied with less than all the pleasure they can get and avoidance of all possible pain. When the emotions dominate our thinking, responsible living is impossible, and so is happiness. This is the danger to affluent America and the greatest danger to Christianity. The clergy is as easily the victim as are people anywhere. They must take the steps required to meet it. The churchmen must learn that money is to be used for the good. It is to be forthrightly and expeditiously used. It is not to be hoarded personally or corporately. Churchmen cannot afford the luxury of money in their pockets when there is so great a demand for it in many urgent ventures with religious significance. Nor can the priest be ever after the people for support in some worthy project if he himself does not believe in it to the degree of making use of all his own possessions to forward the cause. No one can guess the good that would be accomplished if the priests of America made use of their personal funds alone for the work to be done in Latin America. But the Church cannot preach poverty to priests when it accrues great wealth from astute business management.

So many policies of the Church have been dictated by the dollar. The lavish praise of the Church for the work of the missions has not cured the parsimonious attitude of the bishops toward them. The laity is simply not allowed to support the missions to the degree and extent they would wish. The uneconomic use of priests and religious in the classrooms of our schools is the result of miserly thinking. The current situation in our hospitals, where moneymaking dominates the work, allows very little real thought for the poor and needy. The inability of the Church to place its personnel in the vanguard of the war against poverty is another indication of deep involvement in the past and unpreparedness for the present and future tasks. When its personnel is involved in financially productive projects they cannot be taken out of them for the Christian endeavors which demand their talents and dedication. Right now, countless priests and religious should be in training for the apostolate of personal relationships so urgently needed today. Yet, not only are they not available for training, but numbers of them are leaving the work of the Church disenchanted with that work as it is being directed, because of policy largely bound to the dollar. There should be a vast program of training for leaders in the Church. If this task is delayed because those with leader potential cannot be released from the work they are doing now, or enough money is not available to set up such a training program, the Church will lag another hundred years behind. The desirability of education of the masses is no longer debated. The problem now is the education of leaders in and for the Church — priest, brother, nun, and layman. And because of the widespread practice of birth control by the well-to-do and educated, who should provide natural leaders, the situation is all the more critical and urgent. The need for leadership is going to become so critical and urgent that leaders will be sought from every source, including the Church. Real leaders will be listened to as they have never been listened to before if the Church has them ready and available.

Chapter 11

The Foreign Missions

IT IS true to say that nowhere in the Church has *aggiorna-mento* been more urgently needed than in the work of the foreign missions. Nowhere, either, has the spectacle of Church finance been sorrier than in the same foreign missions. Yet Christ's final instructions in the record were to go forth and teach all nations.

The nearly unbelievable facts of history indicate the pathetic lack of knowledge on the part of those making historic decisions for the Church in the foreign missions. That ignorance, understandable when the lack of communications made good decisions very difficult, is incomprehensible now, when marvelous communications can bring accurate information on any situation, in any part of the world, in moments. The foreign missions of the Church continue to be directed and managed in a way worthy of the eighteenth or nineteenth century. The missionary bishops have pleaded, almost in vain, for a sympathetic hearing for their work and their problems. They have gladly eaten the crumbs which fell from the tables of the masters of the Church.

Numerous bishops make available for the missions only the scruffy personnel for which they have no use themselves.

They delegate the theological "seconds" and "thirds" for the underdeveloped Christian nations. When circumstances call for it, they expostulate at length about countries of which they are ignorant, pass judgment on people they do not know, and discuss customs with which they have little sympathy and of which they have even less understanding. They take percentages of collections in their rich dioceses for countries which are poverty-stricken and churchmen who are threadbare. But more than that, they have been quite content to think of missions and missionaries as works and men from another planet, who ought to seek their resources in the places from which they came. If the document *On the Church in the Modern World* quotes the aphorism that he who refuses to feed a starving man kills him, it ought to make plain that the bishops who refuse to feed the starving Church of the missions are killing it. One bishop, without much sense of incongruity, stated to me pointblank that he did not believe in the foreign missions. Were he born totally in ignorance, blind, and stone deaf, this could have been understandable. But the condition persists despite any decree issued or any interest the Holy See may have taken in the missions. Despite the desire of the missionary bishops at the Council to make themselves and their needs known and understood, favorable reaction was negligible.

Neglect of the missions has led almost inevitably to remarkable ingenuity on the part of missionaries, some of whose schemes have brought damage to the Church. When the facts were publicly exposed, the outcry of authority was against the scandal of the publicity. Was the publicity the scandal or were the reprehensible facts?

Some years ago a book was written and published in Shanghai called *Shanghai, Paradise of Adventurers*. Two chapters of this book were devoted to the adventures of the Church in the world of commerce. The missionary Church was merely trying to provide support for its own work. To say that these were not the adventures of the Church but of certain religious orders is to beg the point. They were the adventures of people appointed by their superiors to do an approved job.

An Ordinary, temporarily in Shanghai, deeply resenting this book and its revelations, wanted to refute it with the force of truth. He made contact with one religious order deeply involved in the adventures described. He expected to get the evidence required to settle the calumny with dispatch. Much to his surprise, the religious order involved would have nothing to do with him. He received a "no comment" when he sought the required information. The charges made in the book could not be refuted because they were true. It was as simple as that. If one were to ask why such adventures were considered necessary, the answer would have to be that the financial arteries of the Church were all but closed to the needs of the missions. Despite all Christian teaching and training, few even of the bishops seem to accept that the yellow, red, or black man needing help really is Jesus Christ.

The book mentioned above pointed out the number of merchandizing enterprises in which the Church had money invested. These involved industry, living accommodations, and businesses practicing the very principles condemned by the Church in its encyclicals. The newspapers of Shanghai in the pre-Communist days would report a suicide. Some elderly White Russian had jumped from her apartment window. She had reached the end of her means and the rent had been raised. The last comment in the newspaper story would be, "These apartments were owned by such and such a religious order." And this was not a single incident. It was not unusual to see people in cassocks collecting the rents. One priest in charge of his order's enterprises told me bitterly, "Look at that apartment building. The Church owns it. And we condemn birth control. But only people who practice birth control can live in those apartments. Someday the wrath of God will come down upon us." And it surely did within a very few months, but not before that priest was replaced by the order with another who would take better care of the enterprises and have less to say about them. No one can believe that these religious enjoyed this work, but no one can deny they did it. It was work born of desperation.

Certainly it is not the intention of this writer to rake up scandal after scandal, although it could easily be done. It seems, however, that unless and until a problem appears in print, nothing much is done about it. The management of the finances of the Church is not an easy matter, but since the Church has to be in such work, it should be in it only on the very highest ethical plane. If the Church expects to be heard with some credibility, then it must be easily apparent that its own executives deeply respect the teachings of Christ and are the first to take Him seriously.

What then should be done about the foreign missions? A relative priority in personnel and finance should be fixed by the Church. If there are needy in the world, the Church must be the first to take their plight seriously. If sacrifices are to be made, then the priests and religious must be the first to make them. When it comes to the missions the laity have always been far ahead of the hierarchy in interest, sympathy, and support. In fact, many times rigid controls have been set up to prevent mission societies from getting the support which the people are anxious to give to the missions. It has been said that if Vatican II did one thing for the collective bishops of the Church, it made them realize their responsibility for the whole world, not just each for his own diocese. They may have realized it, but they have so far taken little action.

First of all, the Congregation for the Propagation of the Faith should be headed by a missionary cardinal, not by a papal diplomat. He should be young enough to be very actively in charge. He should realize that the work is more important than himself or his prerogatives. No one can guess the chagrin of missionaries everywhere when the late Cardinal Stritch of Chicago was named head of the congregation. Many missionaries were delighted that an American was named because they hoped that his regime would be typified by American efficiency. However, they were appalled when they learned that he was a dying man being assigned to what should have been a most vital operation.

Diocesan directors for the Society of the Propagation of the Faith should be missionaries with exceptions made only for very able and dedicated men. The job should in no circumstances be a sinecure for a man with virtually no interest in the missions. He should be in direct contact with the missions being helped.

Vocations to the missions should be given top priority. No one should be withheld from the missions with the exception of those honestly considered unfit emotionally for the work.

Every diocese should send priests to the missions, on a voluntary basis only for the more distant and arduous ones, and on a trial basis in closer and more stable ones. They should be sent with, and through, mission-sending societies, structured so as to absorb these men on a temporary basis as associates but still incardinated in their own dioceses and supported by those dioceses. Their work should be undertaken in locations chosen by the home diocese in collaboration with a central planning agency on the national level, and on a sponsorship basis with responsibility for the development of the mission diocese in the best interest of the mission territory.

All mission propaganda should be centralized nationally under the Sacred Congregation in Rome, and managed by highly qualified personnel, religious and lay, supplied by the mission-sending societies. All wasteful overlapping and tasteless promotion work should be eliminated. All gimmickry and promotion schemes for fund raising should be thoroughly examined by a central body of missionaries and associates and implemented or suppressed as desirable. One or two first-class mission periodicals should replace the dreadful and numerous mission appeal magazines, each blowing its own little horn, again, out of desperation.

One central, and as many regional offices as necessary, should be set up to cover all promotion and provision work for the missions.

The laity should be given a large responsibility in mission work under their bishops' direction.

All mission work should be done under the auspices of the Church rather than this or that religious order. All properties and institutions should be under the title of the Church and administered by corporation boards established on local as well as on national levels. The local corporation boards would be subject to the national ones, and the national ones subject to world boards. There must really be world representation on such corporate boards.

The begrudging interest of the bishops of America in the work of the foreign missions, whether they realize it or not, has taken its toll of the clergy at home. When the Church gets to the point of realizing that its vitality at home depends on its interest in the work abroad, something worthwhile will have happened. When even the American government realizes that it simply cannot live in a world in which one half sits in darkness and need, surely the hierarchy of America must have seen the point even earlier, in relation to the Church. If it has not seen it, it is because it has not wanted to, and still does not want to.

Certainly the mood of the people of America seems clearer to the government than to the Church, when the former rather than the latter sends out the Peace Corps. When national aid and goodwill groups are going to Asia, Africa, and Latin America from the secular universities of America, one can only guess at the reasons for the disinterest of the bishops in the Church of the world.

When the Holy Father asked the bishops of America to do something about Latin America, some of them began sending mere token forces of clergy, each from his own diocese. They began an inadequate operation destined from its inception to fail. There are well established foreign mission societies with personnel and experience enough to undertake the direction of this work. Yet these societies have been denied the men and funds they need for imaginative and effective work by the very bishops proud to have their names on their boards. These societies could have expanded the Latin American work under the sponsorship of the bishops, with funds and men supplied by them. But the hearts of the bishops were not in the idea because it involved little or no personal triumph for themselves. Whoever denies the human and understandable, but puerile, need of bishops for adulation denies one of the basic facts of ecclesiastical life.

When the missionary endeavor of the American Church is really vital and strong (and any number of high-powered press releases from sending societies will not make it vital and strong), there will be something to say for the vitality of the American Church. The vitality of the Church cannot be correctly gauged by an impressive collection of brick and mortar monuments to one bishop after another. This gives little credit to a Church called Christian. Many of the people are a little ashamed of the vanity of such leaders. Can men who are not ashamed to build such monuments ever really have an interest in the foreign missions which are so remote from them, where the work is arduous and only modestly successful? Will they care for a work in which the personnel must, if they are to remain sane, forget themselves for others? Hardly. Yet these are the shepherds who by "word and example," as Vatican II expresses it, are to show the way to their sheep. The world is as ready and anxious as it ever was for inspired leadership. It is waiting to respond to the heroism which should be found in the management of the Church. That heroism will be there only when the plight of the missions, and the work of the missions, is of efficacious concern to those in authority in the Church.

Chapter 12

Freedom of Conscience

WITH the exception of direct blasphemy, few sins in the catalog have borne the ignominy surrounding suicide. Most suicides have to be mentally unbalanced. It is obvious that no man should take the life which God has given him. It is just not man's to take; it is his to use and develop. While no one can say for sure that Judas went to hell, Christ was pretty unequivocal in his description of his condition. He were better never born.

Freedom was no less the idea of God than was creation. And, despite all the tyranny of history, and the best motives of the greatest saints in recommending subservience to another for the sake of God, nowhere has God given man permission to repudiate his freedom. Freedom is the very stuff of love, which is man's God-given potential distinguishing him from the apes. Where there is no freedom, there can be no love. And there can be no merit without love. Nor, for that matter, can there be sin or virtue, punishment or reward.

It is nothing short of stunning that the Church, which praised and defended freedom through the ages, did not make a declaration of freedom of conscience until Vatican

II. Opposition did not come because of any doubts about man's inherent, God-given freedom, but rather because of doubts about man's ability to understand and use it well. Surely God appreciated this danger when He gave man freedom in the first place. Real curtailment of man's fundamental freedom is the refusal of a vote of confidence in God. Yet the Church often curtailed freedom in the name of the very author of freedom. How ridiculous can one get! Men have often thought that in so doing, their action was for the best interests of others, but it is generally those people who cannot control themselves who think they know what is best for others.

Because the unlearned have always sought the advice of the educated, it is not surprising that the clergy have been the monitors of the people. Such monitoring is inescapable for children but inexcusable for adults. Obviously, therefore, the Church has for centuries considered most people children. Considering that the mentality of the average TV viewer is that of a twelve year old, perhaps this is reasonable enough. The fact remains that men were born free, and the Church has the serious obligation to teach them how to live and remain free. Morality has been wisely defined as the science of freedom. Yet the Church must accept much blame for standing idly by while the people were robbed of their freedom on many occasions, even though sometimes for apparently good reasons. Certainly the declaration of freedom of conscience is long overdue. But much longer overdue is the need for the Church to teach the use of freedom. As has been said earlier, the tragic mistake of the Church is that it has formed the consciences of too many people and helped too few of them to form their own consciences. Thus, too late has it been discovered that people have been conformists, without having established too much in the way of religious conviction.

The mistakes of the past are coming to light in religious

life. Religious have been encouraged for years to place their freedom in the hands of their superiors, and repudiation of their personal freedom has been praised as the highest form of humility and obedience. Yet now we know that a religious is not justified in repudiating his freedom any more than he is justified in taking his life. For religious obedience can never be true obedience unless it is undertaken with the highest degree of freedom. Obedience is the highest form of love, not a form of slavery. It is the highest form of freedom, not the lowest form of tyranny. Obedience is present when the love of God rules, not when whimsy reigns. Yet so often has the latter been the case, that the very substance of religious obedience is being broadly challenged today.

The desire to help men in spite of themselves has led the Church in the past to threaten them with eternal punishment in the name of God. Yet we know that it is the will of God that all men be saved. We also are very aware that there were no threats issued from the cross against those who crucified the Son of God. There was merely an impassioned and loving prayer from the crucified One to the Father for the deliverance from punishment of those who in ignorance did this terrible thing.

Because of the new dimensions of freedom in the modern world, many have had second and third thoughts about the efficacy of the Church's way of teaching and the value of hastily hurled threats. There must be a proportion between the crime and the punishment. At a time in history when Michigan and many other states make twenty years in prison the maximum sentence for murder, the Church does well to wonder whether there is anything to be gained by the threat of hell for offending Church law. All Church-imposed obligations are coming up for reconsideration in the light of the penalties imposed for failing to fulfill them. This includes not only the obligation to Sunday Mass, but all other obligations right up to and including the celibacy of the clergy. There can never be any doubt about the obligation of the Christian to worship God publicly. The only question about this obligation is whether the failure to do so can be equated with eternal damnation and still be worthy of a God of infinite love and mercy.

The Church, having declared for freedom of conscience, has now given the world notice that it has undertaken the development of personal responsibility in its people. Although long overdue, this step will be only as productive as the people themselves make it. As much will come out of it as is invested in the effort, and the effort is going to call for a great many dedicated people. Now that it is realized that people are not dedicated merely because they take a vow, but rather take a vow because they are dedicated, there will be more care in the selection of those to take the vows, and more responsibility given those who have taken them. There will be more onus on those who take vows to live the virtue after taking the vow. To do this, they must be the freest people in the world, so that they can be the most loving. They must be taught that love is the basic obligation of the Christian, and not something to be considered an occasion of sin. They must learn that the crippling dangers of not loving are far greater than the danger of loving badly. All must have the courage to accept the risks involved in trial and error, and be willing to make the mistakes which are part of the process of learning and living, even in religion. Saying one is a sinner and begging God's forgiveness for sin is not a mere formality but the expression of a true awareness of a fact of life. This whole atmosphere of truth and reality can be developed only when and where there is real freedom and real challenge. The Church, thank God, has declared itself for the future. Now the children have to be encouraged to live freely but to live well. This combination is the assurance of happiness on this earth, where, despite all inferred or implied teaching to the contrary, God did put happiness within the reach of the man who has the courage for purposeful sacrifice.

Finally, the matter of freedom of conscience must not be tied directly to finance. Will the people support the Church, as in the past, if there is no obligation under pain of mortal sin to attend Sunday Mass? It is a moot question and, regardless of the disdain with which some may treat it, a serious and important one. Churchmen should be the first to suspect that, if clarifying the Christian's obligation to worship is a good decision for the Church, it will be a good decision for financing the Church. Deemphasizing the penalty for missing Mass on Sunday would make churchmen work harder to get people to worship God, and certainly their sermons would be better. The problem in making evening Mass available to the people was interwoven with finance. Yet, those who had the courage to think of the good of the people and even of their convenience and comfort, learned very quickly that, though they were not used to having their convenience considered, the people proved themselves grateful and responsive.

All other considerations notwithstanding, the whole matter of freedom of conscience is one in which the Church can not fail to take the lead without at once defaulting its position as a moral force in the world. If its own experience, unequalled in the history of persecution, has not convinced it of this, nothing will. Freedom is God's idea and God's gift, and there can be no question of its primacy or maintenance by any organization under His aegis.

Freedom of conscience is nothing more than the teaching that every man lives or dies eternally by virtue of God's just judgment on his own personal sins. A man can be damned or blessed forever, only as he has, with full knowledge and consent, rejected or accepted God's will as he truly knows it. The Church has always taught this; now it need only practice it.

Chapter 13

The Diaspora

THIS is a very old and meaningful word used to describe the dispersal of the chosen Jewish people in their moments of failure as children of God. They were led into captivity far away from all they called home; they were beaten down and sorely troubled. Karl Rahner is the theologian to whom it appears we owe the application of this term to the Christian Church in the world today. According to him the Church is not a monopolistic organization reigning in a Catholic world, but it is the dispersal of the children of God in a pluralistic society. Therefore, the Church must not operate without taking into consideration the effects of the association of its children with their neighbors. It must look on life and make its laws with due consideration for the ways and thoughts of others.

Failure to do this led, for example, to some of the marriage laws of the Church which have proved so unrealistic and brought such indignation from righteous Christian people. It is ridiculous, in a marriage between a sincere non-Catholic and a Catholic, to require the sincere non-Catholic to sign papers promising to rear his children in a religion which he himself does not accept. The only persons who could sincerely sign such papers would be those who were ignorant of or indifferent to religion or considered one church as good as another. The more sincere the non-Catholic party to such a marriage the more severe the penalty against him. Yet this has gone on for years while the Church rejoiced to some degree in the increment regardless of their worth as believers.

The flaws flowing into Church legislation from the failure to appreciate the significance of the diaspora are very numerous. In the main they have militated against the movement toward Christian unity. Much of this legislation could in no way be justified if examined in the light of charity. And the great scandal of the Christian body has been its lack of charity, one Christian toward the other, let alone Christian toward pagan.

Reorganization of the whole body of Church law must be undertaken with the diaspora in mind. The consciences of the faithful must be safeguarded by clear teachings in this regard. Absolutes must be minimized in law and morality; impossible situations must be recognized for what they really are. The realistic reconciliation of the call to Christian perfection with the state of sinful man must be made, if the growth of man is to be assured and safeguards set up against delusion. There are many facets of Christian living in which countless numbers have been forced into untenable positions, the Church has been made to look ridiculous, and even God Himself has been brought into disrepute by the effrontery of religious men. This must be stopped as quickly as possible.

The only quality which can assure the growth of real religion, charity, is the basic love for truth which is Christ's own guarantee of freedom. If truth is not the weapon of the Christian he is truly defenseless. Suffice it to say that the Church has not always relied on this weapon, but has sometimes resorted to the subterfuges of the world, often appearing to have more confidence in them than in the continuing presence of the spirit of God.

Conclusion

THIS book was intended to present constructive criticism in an urgent situation. Many priests fear that time is running out for their superiors. People are no longer content to wait for solutions in due time; they want them now. They believe there is a middle road between timidity and temerity. They believe there are answers not being given. They are afraid that what can be done will not be done. They are restive, with reason. Many priests feel that although they are not being asked, let alone heard, by their superiors, nevertheless they must speak now or hold their peace forever.

It is not fair to accuse superiors of bad will or no will. But superiors, with few exceptions, seem confused or frightened; most of them don't seem to know what to do. They just don't want the boat rocked. But the sea is rough and the boat is rocking. Regardless of contrary opinion, I have not enjoyed rocking the boat. I have only come to believe, along with many other priests who have given their lives and meager talents to the Church for the work of God, that we have no alternative but to speak up. We have to be heard even if we are rejected.

In the conflict between obedience and authority, which no

one could possibly deny is at the heart of the current confusion, one single sentence expresses the crux of the matter.
It is, "Your superior stands in the place of God for you."
Until now it has been accepted without question, and in an
absolute sense. It has been used as a club to silence those with
the duty to speak. Because of it the best priests and religious
have remained silent in the name of God when the love of
God should have compelled them to speak. It has made safe
cowards of them when actually cowards are never safe.

Can any man really stand in the place of God with all the
limitations of power and prestige that belong to a human
being? Can any man stand in the place of God to a greater
degree than our natural parents? And they have often been
wrong through negligence or undue harshness. Parents have
been rebuked time and again for neglect of their children.
We were never taught that we must give them blind obedience. Many times we have heard that they were not to be
obeyed when they came between our conscience and God.
Is there some difference between the authority of parents and
that of superiors? Who excoriates superiors, as parents are
excoriated, when they do not represent God as they should,
when they are vindictive and venal, or use their office for
their own glory rather than God's? They are supported by
authority lest authority be weakened. Yet what weakens authority more than the flagrant abuse of authority? Children
learn to hate parents who have abused them or deprived them
of true love and affection. And when children develop their
own judgment in adulthood they are no longer under the
strict surveillance of their parents. Are spiritual subjects never
adults? Do superiors never get senile or dotty while still wielding authority enough to make or break good people? Have
they any inherent right, as superiors, to dwarf the judgment
of their subjects who some day must attain sufficient good
judgment to run the Church well?

The idea of anyone standing in the place of God tends to

lessen the image of God as if He could not look after Himself. As if he needed a human stand-in. Surely He can and does use human instruments. But do these human instruments remember that He has chosen the fools of this world to confound the strong, the wise? He Himself was master, but He became the servant. He did not call us servants but friends. Too few superiors have friends. Their insecurity makes friendship difficult for them, for they actually doubt the reality of their representation of God. They need never do so if they would acknowledge its limits.

There are bishops and superiors who are trying with might and main to look ahead to meet and solve the problems of the Church. Since this book was started and before it will be published, much good will have been accomplished. Every priest, religious, or lay person under the direction of these superiors is grateful. Such superiors deserve thanks with full credit and cooperation. They will know how much of what has been written is correct; they may even guess what it cost the writer to set down things which might not be correct. Others may not know. I ask them to believe that I am anxious to help, not hinder, to work with them, not against them, for the people of God, the Church.

Better minds than mine have already said much of what I have said, but I would like to conclude with some specific recommendations:

1. Priests
   a) A massive and thorough talent search should be instituted for the best idea-priests in America, and the most able, to be directed into special fields of development.
   b) There should be established without delay an adequate, well-subsidized, well-staffed religious research center aimed at keeping religion relevant and vital.
2. Seminaries
   a) More objective studies in the curricula. Triumphalism

must be avoided by reemphasizing the divinity of Christ and humanity of the Church.

b) There should be two or three types of seminaries — a very few with the highest academic standards, affiliated or federated with the best universities or colleges, some others with a high-quality faculty and student body, but not necessarily university people, and with a real orientation to the apostolate.

c) All seminaries should be under a national board of bishops, or at least a regional board, so that no one bishop has full say about any seminary.

d) Seminary staffs should be made up of highly qualified religious and lay people, male and female.

3. Bishops

a) All bishops should be named by a national selection committee elected by the national body of bishops, their choice subject to confirmation by Rome. New criteria for selection should be developed.

b) Auxiliary bishops should be chosen by the diocesan clergy, subject to veto by the ordinaries of the ecclesiastical province.

c) There should be more dioceses with more bishops with executive power.

d) Diocesan consultors should be named by the bishop and his pastors, two-thirds by the ordinary and one-third by the priests.

e) Deans should be elected by the priests of the deanery for a specific period of time.

f) Each diocese should have a disciplinary committee to handle all personnel discipline, three members to be named by the bishop and two elected by the priests of the diocese.

g) There should be regional courts of appeal against the injustices of authority, with independent judges, to assure fair examination of causes and impartiality of verdicts.

h) There should be an audit of all ecclesiastical finances available to anyone with cause to seek it. Areas of financial priority ought to be determined by committee.

4. Pastors

a) The laity should be widely used on the parish level to relieve priests for strictly pastoral work. Pastoral committees should function in every diocese, but meaningless societies should be eliminated.

b) Suitable spirituality for diocesan clergy must replace the monastic spirituality of the past. Celibacy should be thoroughly and realistically restudied, as well as the economical use of priests and the problems of materialism, legalism, and situational conflicts.

5. Canon law

a) There is a tremendous urgency for the earliest possible revision, oriented to charity.

b) Canon law must be people-oriented, using the "All power is given to me" of Christ, on behalf of souls. There must be free use of fallible judgment, without apology in court cases and legal matters, such as marriage cases, and such as was used in the Pauline Privilege, as well as the Privilege of the Faith in the early days.

6. Liturgy

a) Maximum room must be made for free forms of worship around the central act of the sacrifice of the Mass.

b) New avenues must be found for the flow of worship into the daily lives of the people, in domestic, business, and social areas.

7. Catholic education

a) Schools as well as hospitals must not be allowed to devour the professionally dedicated religious of the

Church. Personnel is more important than money in making decisions in this field.

b) Work should proceed toward a federation or association of public, government-supported, religious schools for those children whose parents wish them to have a religious education.

8. Foreign missions

a) There should no longer be any foreign missions in the former sense of the word, in a shrunken world where the Church is the responsibility of all the bishops. All missions should be budgeted for by all dioceses and administrated as parts of dioceses.

b) Eighty percent of the mission personnel should be laity, in works hierarchically but not clerically dominated.

The Questionnaire

QUESTIONNAIRES and statistics can be used to prove almost anything; they often prove nothing. The following may at least prove interesting. The questions were purposefully asked but only sometimes purposefully answered. Those answered thoughtfully were often less truthful or unbiased than those answered without deliberation.

This questionnaire was sent to men known for their interest in the Church. Apparently, too short a limit was set on the time to make reply. Two hundred twenty questionnaires went out and eighty-nine were returned. The widest response came from pastors of ten to fifteen years' experience (47%).

The replies represent the following archdioceses and dioceses:

Boston	New York	Buffalo
Chicago	Philadelphia	Calgary
Cincinnati	St. Louis	Camden
Detroit	St. Paul	Crookston
Dubuque	San Antonio	Davenport
Indianapolis	San Francisco	Des Moines
Los Angeles	Toronto	Duluth
Louisville	Washington	Duluth
Milwaukee	Albany	Ferns
Newark	Amarillo	Fort William
		Green Bay

Hamilton	Nassau, Bahamas	Saginaw
Kansas City	Natchez-Jackson	St. Augustine
(St. Joseph)	Ogdensburg	Sault Ste. Marie
London, Can.	Oklahoma City-Tulsa	Sioux Falls
Manchester	Providence	Springfield, Ill.
Miami	Rochester	Toledo
Nashville	Rockville Centre	

INTERESTING OBSERVATIONS ON
THE QUESTIONNAIRE

Those who answered:
> 72% are pastors and have been for over ten years.
> 71% are over forty years of age.

Opinions expressed:
> 83% are enthusiastic about Vatican II.
> 79% anticipate profound effects from it.
> 82% believe their people are pleased with the new liturgy.
> 74% believe the clergy is pleased with the new liturgy.
> 84% agree that present parishes are too large.
> 73% want more dioceses formed.
> 74% think radical change is needed in the curial setup.
> 93% want more assurance that competent priests will have a voice in diocesan councils and planning.
> 87% favor priest-elected representatives on bishops' councils.
> 61% feel they have easy access to their ordinary.
> 48% consider their chanceries to be adequate and cooperative.
> 80–84% desire less pomp and ring-kissing and a restriction of empty honors.
> 67% favor abolition of monsignori — not their physical extinction.
> 85% believe moderate to radical changes are required in seminary training.
> 72% feel that pastoral training is inadequate.
> 73% favor celibacy in the priesthood as it is now.
> 82% favor facilities for honorable dispensation from celibacy.
> 38% believe no unusual trend has been shown toward married clergy; 42% believe there has.
> 78% would allow married convert ministers to be ordained.
> 84% feel that Catholic education is only a qualified success.

70% think that it should receive government aid.

89% think that the best qualified religious should be teaching religion.

81% think that religious women should be more involved in parish work.

76–79% think that the present system of provision for the foreign missions is wasteful and inadequate, and that there should be some effective central system to handle personnel, money, and materials for mission work.

The questionnaire itself follows for those wishing to note other opinions expressed, as well as the areas covered by the questionnaire. Percentages are based on the total number who answered each particular question.

CLERGY QUESTIONNAIRE

I am a pastor 72%   curate 16%   and have been for less than
    5 years 7%   10 years 23%   15 years 24%   20 years 9%
    25 years 12%   more than 25 years 17%
I am under 30 years of age 1%   40 16%   50 23%   60 38%
    over 60 years of age 10%
My archdiocese 37%   diocese 54%   is . . . . .

A. VATICAN COUNCIL II

1. Re Vatican II, are you enthusiastic 83%   disappointed 3% indifferent 6%?

2. Would you prefer it to run longer 31%   shorter 1% stop now 58%?

3. Will its effects be profound 79%   superficial 9% negligible 23%?

4. Will Catholics and fervor increase 63%   decrease 1% stabilize 23%?

B. THE CHURCH

I. The Liturgy

1. Are your people pleased 82%   displeased 7%   by the new liturgy? indifferent 7%   confused 11%?

2. Are the priests in your parish enthusiastic 74%   unmoved 8%   indifferent 8%   about the new liturgy?

3. Was the move too fast 23%   too slow 11%   timely 58%?

II. Discipline

1. Do you think most present Church discipline should be made voluntary and spiritually motivated rather than penal?
   Yes 60%   No 23%

Friday abstinence	Yes 58%	No 34%
Sunday Mass	Yes 35%	No 61%
Lenten regulations	Yes 66%	No 34%
Divine office	Yes 45%	No 51%
Easter duty	Yes 48%	No 47%

2. Do you think the development of individual conscience and personal responsibility in the Church has been a failure 51% a success 24%?

III. The Human Church

1. Do you think statistics have been

necessary 25%	realistic 5%	helpful 31%
overdone 26%	unrealistic 21%	detrimental 7%

2. Do you think financial aspects have been handled

well 24%	indifferently 10%	responsibly 14%
badly 21%	autocratically 33%	wastefully 10%
unjustly ...	whimsically 15%	purposefully 8%

3. Do you think accounting for funds used by the Church has been

   generally good 28%   poor 31%   mediocre 34%

4. Do you think the juridical Church has been

realistic 9%	too technical 25%
unrealistic 20%	too legalistic 60%
deterrent 15%	responsible 12%
cumbersome 31%	spiritually stimulating 1%

5. Do you think the spiritual Church has been

spiritual 24%	unvaried 21%	too rubrical 31%
devotional 36%	too varied 17%	legal 26%

IV. Catholic Education

1. Do you think it is a qualified 84%   unqualified 10% success?

too costly 31%   reasonable 23%?
should have government aid 70%?
first-rate 25%   second-rate 54%   third-rate 6%?
teaches religion well 20%   badly 20%   indifferently 35%?
makes for ghetto mentality 23%?
is wasteful of priest power 43%?

2. Do you think the Church has failed secular education?
Yes 31%   No 57%   by keeping students and catholicity
away from public schools 7%   public high schools 12%
colleges and universities 18%?

3. Do you think the best-qualified religious should be teaching
religion?   Yes 89%   No 2%
teaching in public educational institutions?   Yes 39%
No 2%   Some 48%

4. Do you think the cost of Catholic education could be better
applied to other works of the Church, in view of the general
availability of public education?   Yes 36%   No 29%
Doubtful 30%

5. Do you think the laity is used well 24%   badly 26%
indifferently 39%   in Catholic schools?

V. The Mission Church

1. Do you think Catholic America's approach to foreign missions
is adequate 17%   inadequate 73%?

2. Do you think there should be a central organization making personnel, money, and materials available?   Yes 76%
No 10%

3. Do you think the present proliferation of effort, societies,
and appeals is adequate 12%   inadequate 27%   wasteful
52%?

4. Do you consider foreign mission propaganda good 24%
bad 8%   indifferent 44%   embarrassing 17%?

5. Do you think diocesan priests should go to foreign missions?

all 3%	some countries 20%
a quota 14%	one year 8%
volunteers 70%	five years 20%
any place 24%	as long as they wish 60%

C. THE HIERARCHY

I. The Pope

1. Do you think the Council has increased 69% decreased 8% had no effect 19% on the bond of unity and respect for the pope in the USA?

2. Do you think the curial setup is helpful 10% harmful 12% as good as could be expected 14% needs radical change 74%?

3. Do you think more decisive administrative power should be exercised? Yes 45% No 8%
nationally 44% regionally 45%

II. The Bishop

1. Do you think the present system of episcopal appointments is adequate 16% inadequate 51% as good as any 25%?

2. Would you favor election by priests 35%?
dismissal or retirement on a two-thirds vote of priests?
Yes 34% No 47%
mandatory retirement age? Yes 61% No 34%

3. Do you think episcopal power, as presently generally exercised, allows too much latitude? Yes 37% No 39%
allows adequate appeal? Yes 25% No 45%
allows for too much whimsy? Yes 57% No 18%

4. Would you favor regional courts of appeal, under independent priest-judges, to hear claims of priests or religious against unjust or discriminatory treatment? Yes 61% No 25%
for laity with the same claims? Yes 58% No 24%

5. Do you favor less pomp? Yes 80% No 2%
restriction of ring-kissing to ceremonial? Yes 84% No 7%
restriction of empty honors? Yes 83% No 5%
abolition of monsignori? Yes 67% No 21%
more dioceses 73% fewer dioceses 2%?

6. Would you like more assurance of the voice of competent priests being heard in diocesan councils and planning?
Yes 93% No 2%

7. Do you favor priest-elected representatives on bishops' councils? Yes 87% No 7%
elections of deans by priests of the deaneries? Yes 69% No 20%

8. Have you easy access to your ordinary?   Yes 61%   No 19%
   reasonable access?   Yes 34%   No 5%

III. The Chancery

1. Do you consider your chancery adequate 48%   inadequate
   23%   cooperative 48%   authoritarian 18%   cumber-
   some 17%?

2. Do you consider emanations from the chancery realistic 42%
   unrealistic 30%   too frequent 21%   too detailed 10%

IV. The Priest

1. Do you consider seniority the best method of appointment?
   Yes 23%   No 69%

2. Do you think pastors should periodically be changed?
   Yes 64%   No 21%

3. Do you think pastoral training adequate 17%   inadequate
   72%?

4. Do you think priests generally
   have too much money 21%   are too lazy 24%
   drink too much 21%   work too hard 12%
   have too much leisure 17%

5. Do you favor celibacy as it is now?   Yes 73%   No 18%
   voluntary 25%   obligatory 44%?
   any married clergy?   Yes 38%   No 42%
   ordaining married convert ministers?   Yes 78%   No 10%
   older Catholic business or professional married men?
   Yes 54%   No 27%
   reinstatement of any married ex-priests?   Yes 54%   No 29%
   Do you favor facilities for the honorable dispensation of
   priests from celibacy?   Yes 82%   No 9%
   to continue as priests?   Yes 30%   No 54%

6. Do you think present parishes are too big?   Yes 84%
   No 9%

7. Do you think any diocesan priest should have pastor status
   after twenty years?   Yes 65%   No 15%

D. SEMINARIES

I. Training

1. Do you think present training adequate 21%   inadequate
   63%?

2. Do you think a change is needed?   radical 43%   moderate 42%   none 2%

3. Do you think the shortage of priests is realistic 29%?   too many in nonpriestly work 62%?

4. Do you think the shortage of vocations is due to uninspiring priests 43%   unhappiness in priesthood 12%   affluent society 65%   indifference to religion 29%   failure of Catholic education 18%?

5. Do you thing seminary discipline is adequate 21%   inadequate 18%   unreasonable 5%   badly handled 17%   immaturely administered 34%   obsolete 25%?

6. What ails the seminary course?
   too long 3%   too short 3%
   badly chosen staff 24%
   ivory tower mentality 33%
   spoon-fed 26%   no dialogue 37%
   taught badly 21%   by wrong people 24%

7. What about moral theology for confessional purposes?
   too objective 34%
   fails to consider subjectivity of guilt and malice 40%
   does not form conscience with freedom 29%
   based on unrealistic distinctions 26%
   makes venial and mortal sin too arbitrary 27%

8. Requirements for candidates?
   adequate 43%   inadequate 23%
   Psychological testing?
   adequate 12%   inadequate 47%
   Preparation for celibacy?
   adequate 26%   inadequate 47%

9. Are preparatory seminaries desirable 24%   undesirable 47%   inevitable 10%?

E. RELIGIOUS

I. Priests

1. Do you think the relationship between religious and secular priests is good 38%   poor 20%   mediocre 38%?

2. Do you think religious priests should be more involved pastorally?   Yes 62%   No 29%

3. Do you thing religious orders are too numerous?   Yes 63%
No 18%
Should some be dissolved because their purpose no longer
exists?   Yes 60%   No 9%

4. Do religious get too great a proportion of vocations?   Yes
21%   No 44%

5. Do you think religious too worldly?   Yes 30%   No 37%

II. Religious Women

1. Do you consider the relationship of secular priests with religious women to be good 36%   bad 18%   indifferent 44%
Is it the fault of the Sisters 48%   priests 43%?

2. Do you think Sisters are too restricted?   Yes 76%   No 16%
uncooperative?   Yes 16%   No 45%
immature?   Yes 36%   No 23%
depersonalized?   Yes 56%   No 24%
should be more involved in parish work?   Yes 81%   No 8%
are neglected spiritually and academically by priests?   Yes
72%   No 10%
want closer association?   Yes 40%   No 24%

3. Do you think the training of Sisters makes them mature,
responsible, effective people?   Yes 29%   No 56%

4. What causes the shortage of vocations to the Sisterhood?

uninspiring life 33%   conformism 27%
too much restriction 37%   failure to modernize 44%
symptomatic of times 39%   too great demands for numbers
too great pressures 17%   8%

F. THE LAITY

I. Church Work

1. Do you think the laity should be used in much more 46%
some more 28%   of the administrative work of the Church
now done by priests?

2. Do you think lay advisory boards on the parish level are
mandatory 30%   advisable 42%   desirable 27%   should
be forbidden 2%?

II. Personally

1. Do you think there is rebellion against the Church?
Yes 24%   No 65%

2. Do you think birth control should be left to conscience because of deep conflicts and unfathomable circumstances?
Yes 36%   No 34%
Do you think birth control admits of veniality?   Yes 27%
No 20%
Do you favor open discussion of the problem?   Yes 61%
No 20%

3. Do you think marriage regulations are too strict and unrealistic?   Yes 46%   No 31%
Do you think marriage courts should favor persons rather than laws in questions of real doubt?   Yes 72%   No 11%
Do you think doubts should favor persons 46%   or the sacrament 17%

4. Do you think marriage by the following is mostly invalid?
teen-agers?   Yes 21%   No 56%
alcoholics?   Yes 26%   No 42%
emotionally retarded? Yes 46%   No 21%
subsequent psychopaths?   Yes 35%   No 26%